GUIDELINES FOR SELECTING BIAS-FREE TEXTBOOKS AND STORYBOOKS

COUNCIL ON INTERRACIAL BOOKS FOR CHILDREN

1841 Broadway, New York, N.Y. 10023

© Council on Interracial Books for Children, Inc.
(for original materials only)

Library of Congress Catalog Card Number 80-16903
ISBN # 0-930040-33-3

CONTENTS

ACKNOWLEDGMENTS	v
ABOUT THE GROUP THAT PREPARED THESE GUIDELINES	1
ON USING THESE GUIDELINES	2
TERMINOLOGY AND DEFINITIONS	3
BIAS IN CHILDREN'S STORYBOOKS	7
Introduction	7
Towards Positive Human Values	9
Storybook Rating Instrument	23
Ten Quick Ways to Analyze Children's Books for Racism and Sexism	24
BIAS IN TEXTBOOKS	27
Introduction	27
Underrepresentation	28
Ideal vs. Real	29
Bias in Basal Readers	30
Sexism in Basal Readers and other Textbooks, Too	31
Racism in Basal Readers and other Textbooks, Too	39
AfroAmericans	46
Asian Americans	50
Latinos	53
Native Americans	56
Handicapism in Basal Readers	59
Ageism in Basal Readers	63
More Problems in Textbooks	66
The Influence of Textbooks	68
California Criteria for the Evaluation of Instructional Materials	70
Checklist for Basal Readers	73
Checklist for Literature Anthologies	75
Checklist for Dictionaries	77
Checklist for Biographies	78
Checklist for Math Textbooks	79
Checklist for Bilingual Textbooks	81
Checklist for Career Education Textbooks	83
BIAS IN U.S. HISTORY TEXTBOOKS	86
Introduction	86
Examples of History Text Bias	92
Checklists	96
AVAILABLE MATERIALS	104

ACKNOWLEDGMENTS

In late 1979, the U.S. Office of Education invited the Council on Interracial Books for Children to make a presentation on bias-free guidelines to program officers at HEW. The presentation aroused considerable interest. Many in the audience urged that the guidelines developed by the Council be assembled in print so that they, and other educators, might have a practical tool to evaluate learning materials for possible bias. Grace E. Watson, director of the Horace Mann Learning Center where the presentation took place, encouraged the Council to proceed in this venture.

The task of compiling the guidelines was made easier because of the work of Bonnie Kepplinger and her associates at Scott, Foresman & Co. on a similar project. The Council had served as a consultant to the Scott, Foresman project (which was to prepare guidelines for their editors and authors). We are grateful to Scott, Foresman for permission to draw heavily on those unpublished guidelines.

While Grace E. Watson and Bonnie Kepplinger played key roles in the events that led to the publication of this book—and we extend to them our warmest thanks—the responsibility for the final content is strictly our own.

We believe this book constitutes the Council's most important contribution to date, and it is appropriate at this time to express our gratitude to the many reviewers and writers—too numerous to mention—who have written for the *Bulletin* and other Council publications during the past 15 years. The perspectives of these reviewers—people of color, feminists of all colors, disability rights activists, anti-ageism activists, and other members of oppressed groups—have provided the insights and perspectives upon which these guidelines are based. The research of Drs. Jeana Wirtenberg of the National Institute of Education, and Patricia B. Campbell of William Paterson College has also been most helpful.

ABOUT THE GROUP THAT PREPARED THIS VOLUME

The Council on Interracial Books for Children was founded in 1966 by writers, editors, illustrators, teachers, librarians and parents committed to effecting basic change in books and other children's media. Council programs are designed to promote learning materials that embody the principles of cultural pluralism and are free of sexist, racist, ageist or handicapist bias.

The Council publishes the Interracial Books for Children *Bulletin*, featuring critical analyses of racist and sexist stereotypes prevalent in children's books and learning materials. The *Bulletin* reviews new children's books and educational materials, publishes the findings of Council studies and research projects, and recommends materials for combatting racism and sexism in the home, in the library, and in the classroom.

A division of the Council is the *Racism and Sexism Resource Center for Educators*. The Resource Center develops filmstrips, books, lesson plans and teaching strategies to achieve bias-free education. The Center also provides consultants, conducts in-service training programs for schools, churches and publishers, and cooperates with community groups in consciousness-raising activities. A catalog listing all materials and services of the Resource Center will be sent on request.

Council on Interracial Books for Children

ON USING THESE GUIDELINES

All buyers of children's books use guidelines, whether or not they realize it, and whether or not the guidelines appear in print. Buyers look for appealing stories, or excellent writing quality, for beautiful art, or easy-to-read print. Some buyers are concerned about strong paper and sturdy binding. Others care about teaching methodology, high interest level, or objectivity of viewpoint. All of these guidelines are important. And all involve inevitable value judgments on the part of the book buyer—judgments which may be more informed if the buyer has been trained as a librarian, as a curriculum or reading specialist, or as a graphic art specialist. All kinds of undergraduate and graduate courses are offered for this training.

But where do book buyers turn to become more informed about another important issue in children's books—the issue of biased content? A mere handful of colleges and universities offer courses on topics like "Sexism and Racism in Learning Materials." This means that very few parents or educators have access to such training. So how do we go about developing bias-free children?

Because the first storybooks children read or hear are so important in shaping their self-image and their images of others—and because textbooks continue that process and are key to a child's attitudes and knowledge—guidelines on issues of bias are as vital to book buyers as are guidelines on literary merit, art, paper quality, or methodology.

As long as bias exists in society it will be reflected in books, including children's books. As long as bias exists we must learn to counteract it, no matter how subtly it cloaks its harmful messages. This book of guidelines reflects the Council's desire to share its 15 years of experience with others wishing to eliminate bias in books.

The guidelines were years in preparation because the group preparing them had to learn slowly—learn from one another and from activists in many areas. Whites had a lot to learn about bias against people of color. Blacks had a lot to learn about bias against Asian Americans, Latinos and Native Americans—and vice versa. Non-disabled had to learn about bias against disabled people. Younger people had to learn about bias against older people. Men learned from women about sex bias. And all members of the Council learned a great deal from other groups who were doing similar work.

In sharing our insights we in no way mean to imply that our guidelines are perfect, or final, or foolproof, or to be followed unquestioningly. On the contrary, we urge readers to read with a critical, questioning mind. Question the guidelines, yes. But also question your own past assumptions, your own stereotypes, your own cultural perspectives. These perspectives may be more limiting than you realized.

The guidelines are not meant to be prescriptive. We ask that they be used to understand perspectives different from your own and, in that way, to broaden and enrich your own life and the lives of the children who will learn from the books you carefully select.

TERMINOLOGY AND DEFINITIONS

Our terminology is inconsistent, political, and evolving. We state this not as an apology, but in the belief that the same holds true for everyone's terminology.

Language, reflecting society, is not static. It is no more sacred than anything else in the socio-political arena. In our racist and sexist society, our decisions about word usage are political decisions. When one uses the male pronoun to mean both sexes, one is—consciously or unconsciously—making a political statement. Likewise, the use of the outmoded terms "Negro" or "Colored" today has clear political connotations. Both the words we use and their connotations are in a constant state of change as our society's consciousness of racism and sexism develops.

Language not only expresses ideas and concepts, but it actually shapes thought. If one accepts that our dominant white culture is racist, then one would expect our language—an indispensable transmitter of culture—to be racist as well. Whites, as the dominant group, are not subjected to the same abusive characterization by our language that people of color receive. Similarly, in this male dominated society, demeaning language falls disproportionately on females.

This book upper cases "Black" when it is used as a proper noun to represent "African American." When "white" stands for a class of people and is used as a common noun to represent "white American," it is lower-cased. Should we speak of a particular group of white Americans, such as Polish Americans, we would of course use the capital letter.

Other terminology is still in a state of flux. For example, this book reflects the current confusion on the designation of the original inhabitants of this continent as "Native Americans," or "Native Peoples," as against "American Indians," or "Indians"—and of their particular group as a "nation" or "people" as against "tribe." Many Native Americans *do* use "Indian" and "tribe" in referring to their own people. However, many other Native Peoples suggest that "Indian," "tribe" and a host of similar words are incorrect and also carry derogatory connotations in our society.

Words which sound stilted or "funny" to us one day become comfortable in a short time—if we are truly determined to rid our language and our society of sexism and racism.

The linguist Benjamin Whorf has pointed out that language is more than a reflection of the structural arrangements of communication in society; it is intimately linked to the creation and perception of reality itself. Eliminating biased terminology is one concrete way to change and to correct the way we view ourselves and others.

To conclude, using words as a political tool is a mind-stretching exercise. We recommend it.

The following are definitions of terms as used in this book:

AGEISM: Any attitude, action or institutional practice which subordinates people based upon their age. While ageism results in distorted views of older people by young people, its more serious consequences are to keep many older people in U.S. society severely impoverished, to exclude them from satisfying work and to treat them as useless, unwanted and unattractive citizens.

ASIAN AMERICANS: Refers to people of Asian descent living in the United States. ("Oriental" is considered a pejorative word because it evokes images of the "exotic Orient"—a land of spices, silk and jade. Similarly, "Asiatic" evokes images of hordes of foreigners—of the "Yellow Peril." It has been used so often with negative connotations that it is a term to avoid.)

BLACKS: African Americans. We spell with an upper-case "B" because we use the term in this book as a proper noun to refer to a specific group of U.S. citizens, African Americans. When we refer to a specific group of white U.S. citizens, e.g., Polish Americans, Irish Americans, we capitalize the words as proper nouns. When we generalize about whites in the United States we follow the common noun, lower-case usage. When we generalize about black people, i.e. African Americans, Africans and Papua New Guineans, we also follow the common noun, lower-case usage and use the lower case "b."

CLASSISM: Any attitude, action or institutional practice which subordinates people due to their economic condition. In the United States, poor people and members of the working class are not accorded the dignity and respect (let alone the economic rewards) accorded to wealthy upper-class people. See also "elitism."

CULTURAL RACISM: The imposition of one race's culture in such a way as to withhold respect for, to demean or to destroy the cultures of other races. White European culture has assumed—and has used its institutions to enforce—the superiority of its own culture, values, religions, styles of art, languages and perspectives. At the same time, it has derogated the values, religions, styles of art, languages, and perspectives of Blacks, Asian Americans, Native Americans (Indians) and Latinos.

CULTURAL SEXISM: The imposition of stereotyped sex roles on each generation by society's institutions—families, schools, churches, television, newspapers, etc. An individual's capabilities are submerged by socially acceptable expectations of behavior deemed "masculine" and behavior deemed "feminine." While males in addition to females have been victimized by this process, "masculine" roles are more highly valued and are given a more positive status by most societies. Women's identity and self-concept in U.S. society have been based primarily on their role as sex objects, or in serving positions or in nurturing and self-sacrificing family relationships. This has served to subordinate women and to deny the development of their full human potential.

ELITISM: Any attitude, action or institutional practice which subordinates people due to their social position, economic class or lifestyle. The belief held by people in power that they are superior to those without power. Snobbishness.

ETHNOCENTRISM: The belief that one's own race and culture are superior.

EUROCENTRISM: The consideration of events and people exclusively from the perspective of whites who came to the United States from Europe.

FEMINIST: An advocate for the full rights of women. (Feminists can be male as well as female.)

HANDICAPISM: Any attitude, action or institutional practice which subordinates people due to their disability. Handicapist institutional practices prevent the integration of disabled people into the mainstream of society and keep them socially and economically oppressed.

HERO: Any heroic person, male or female. We deliberately avoid "feminine" word endings because, historically, such suffixes have been used to connote something "lesser than" the male meanings.

HISPANIC: See *Latino*.

INSTITUTIONAL RACISM: Institutional arrangements of a society used to benefit a particular race, at the expense of other races. Institutional racism can be intentional or unintentional. When one race dominates the major institutions of a society, that race has the power to impose its prejudice to the detriment of other races. Because U.S. institutions have always been controlled by whites, racism—in the United States—is white racism. Minority people, in the United States, have no control over institutions. Therefore, there is no such thing as "black racism" or "reverse racism" *in this country*. Of course, people of color can be prejudiced, just as white people, but without control of institutional power to subordinate white people, they cannot be racists.

INSTITUTIONAL SEXISM: Institutional arrangements of a society used to benefit one sex at the expense of the other. Institutional sexism can be intentional or unintentional. The control of institutional power by males has put them in a position of dominance over females and has allowed them to exploit women's labor and to deny women equal access and opportunities within a wide range of institutional settings; e.g., government, business, employment, education, religion, etc.

LATINO or
LATINO AMERICAN: Refers to Chicanos (Mexican Americans), to Puerto Ricans (living in the United States), and to some people from Central American, South American or Caribbean countries living in the United States. *Hispanics* is another term often used to describe these groups. However, those who prefer to be known as *Latinos* say that word was coined to express a common cultural heritage (Black, Native American and Spanish), while *Hispanic* merely reflects common usage of a European based language.

MINORITY: See *third world*.

NATIVE AMERICAN: Refers to descendants of the original peoples who inhabited this continent prior to their conquest by Europeans. This book also uses the terms *Indians* and *Native People*. Recommended usage is to refer to a particular people or nation by name (e.g., Cherokee, Hopi).

NEO-COLONIAL: The "new form" of colonialism that exists after a colony achieves political and governmental independence from the colonizing country but remains economically dependent. Neo-colonized nations do not control their own wealth, resources and industry, and they are still basically controlled from outside.

PREJUDICE: An attitude, opinion, or feeling formed without adequate prior knowledge, thought or reason. Prejudice can be prejudgment for or against any person, group, sex or object.

RACE or
SEX PREJUDICE: Usually involves positive attitudes toward one's own race or sex and negative attitudes toward other races, and to the other sex. People belonging to any race or either sex can be prejudiced.

RACISM: Race prejudice *plus* the back-up of institutional *power,* used to the advantage of one race and the disadvantage of other races. The critical concept differentiating racism from prejudice is "the back-up of institutional power." Racism is any attitude, action or institutional practice—backed up by institutional power—which subordinates people because of their color.

SEXISM: Sex prejudice *plus* the back-up of institutional power to impose that prejudice, used to the advantage of one sex and the disadvantage of the other. Sexism is any attitude, action or institutional practice—backed up by institutional power—which subordinates people because of their sex.

SUBORDINATE: To relegate to a lower rank or class. To oppress.

THIRD WORLD: Refers to people in the United States who are often called "minority" or "non-white." While people of color *are* a minority in this country, they are the vast majority of the world's population, and white people are a distinct minority. Use of the term "minority" ignores the global majority/minority reality—a fact of increasing importance in the interconnected liberation struggles of people of color inside and outside the United States. Use of the term results in our losing sight of this reality. (To describe people of color as "non-white" is to use whiteness as the standard or "norm" against which all others are defined. It is doubtful that whites would appreciate being defined as "non-colored.")

BIAS IN CHILDREN'S STORYBOOKS

(credit note: The following section is adapted from the introduction to the book Human (and Anti-Human) Values in Children's Books, *published by the Council in 1976. For availability of the book, see p. 104.)*

Children's books are not merely a matter of text (which may be lively, entertaining, and stirring, or not) plus pictures (which may be well-done or not). Children's books are not merely exciting, imaginative, and full of good characters or the opposite. No; Hugh Lofting's modest *Doctor Dolittle* is actually a very political and colonialist fellow and *Bright April* by Marguerite De Angeli sets forth an entire ideology of passively "turning the other cheek" in her quiet way. No writer is just a reporter, and artists put more on paper than their eyes see.

Most of us who work with children's literature know this. We realize that children's books do carry a message—a moral, a value or set of values—and that they mold minds. But how often do we stop to consider the source of those values? Do they come from the personal beliefs of the writer? Do they come from the publisher's mind? If so, then we must ask in the persistent way of children themselves: where do *their* values come from?

We propose that those values are not simply individual, not creatures of a series of vacuums, but that they rise from the total society. In any given society, children's books generally reflect the needs of those who dominate that society. A major need is to maintain and fortify the structure of relations between dominators and dominated. The prevailing values are supportive of the existing structure; they are the dominator's values.

We further propose that children's books play an active part in maintaining that structure by molding future adults who will accept it. Today, we see how such books can also mold human beings with counter-values that may help to restructure the society. Children's books are both mirror and matrix.

Stop right there, some will say; you are talking about brainwashing. It is only in totalitarian societies that books are used by a class of people to suit its purposes; in a democracy, books just reflect the interests of the majority. Sad to say, examination of thousands of children's books published in the United States over the years does not bear up this belief. The value-system that dominates in them is very white, very contemptuous of females except in traditional roles, and very oriented to the needs of the upper classes. It is geared to individual achievement rather than to community well-being. It is a value-system that can serve only to keep people of color, poor people, women, and other dominated groups "in their place" because, directly or indirectly, it makes children—our future adults—think that this is the way things should be. So powerful is that system that authors can write *totally unaware* of its influence upon them. More often than not, they are unconscious tools of that system.

If all this seems shocking, let us stop to think: how often have we attended a wedding ceremony and never stopped to think about those words: "I now pronounce you man and wife." Why *man* and *wife,* which reduces the female to a person defined by her relation to another, while the male retains his independent identity? And how many of us speak of a day of woe as "a black day," without

The Story of Doctor Dolittle (1920) was the first of many Dolittle books. The second won the Newbery Medal. The books demean Indians and Blacks, as witness King Koko, above. "Ludicrous, vain" Koko sends the first letter by Swallow Mail to a friend "who runs a shoeshine parlor in Alabama."

realizing that those words equate black with bad and thus help to perpetuate racism? There is a whole world of conditioning and control around us that most people have still to perceive. This is not to say that words in themselves can be the cause of sexism or racism; they only reflect those realities. But they are important, for they condition people—especially children—to accept the maintenance of sexism and racism.

Let's make it also clear that we have no desire to see children's books that would solely help the dominated get a bigger piece of the pie. We don't like the pie, period. Very often, for example, the study of "women's accomplishments" in history has a give-me-more-pie approach and fails to question the very definition of "accomplishments." We should not study merely the few women who have overcome sexist barriers, but examine the very standards that have excluded other women's actions from being considered "accomplishments." We are not interested in seeing different people win a place in the status quo, the present social structure. We are challenging the structure itself because it promotes anti-human values.

The most famous of Lofting's African characters is Prince Bumpo who dreams of turning white to win the Sleeping Beauty who spurned him because of his color. While such blatant racism no longer pervades children's literature, the Dolittle books still circulate widely and influence children.

There is one more important point, and it is closely related to the previous ones. We propose that most of what has been labelled *human nature* in our society really should be called *culturally conditioned behavior*. There is the popular assumption that jealousy, possessiveness, competitiveness, and war (between nations, peoples, classes, and sexes) are inevitable because of the invisible, all-powerful force called human nature. Yet actual experience, in the United States and other countries, shows that those human tendencies assumed to be immutable are in fact variable. If we did not believe that most *human nature* is in fact *cultural conditioning,* there would be little point in publishing this book. If we assumed that human beings are doomed to continue harming and destroying each other without end, there would be no point at all. But we do not hold that assumption; we firmly believe that when the cultural environment is changed, people will change. We reject that vision of the future which portrays human beings as oxen forever yoked to the painful weight of so-called *human nature*. We reject it for the sake of our own lives and, above all, for the generations of children now and tomorrow.

This view of life is not some impossible dream. History has shown that value-systems, like social systems, are not static. Human values change when society changes, and because society changes.

The last decade in the United States has seen strong pressures on the society to change, to become less oppressive for large groups of people. These pressures, in turn, have brought major upheavals in concepts about social relations. If many people now realize there is something wrong with phrases like a *black day* or *man and wife,* it is because Black people and women, as groups, have strongly challenged the status quo and its values.

Concepts about race and sex relationships are the major areas of upheaval today, but we have also seen other challenges. People—mostly young people—have questioned our dog-eat-dog, materialistic lifestyle. Older people have spoken out against the idea that the word *old* should be equated with the forgotten, the useless, the half-witted. And disabled people have been claiming their right to be mainstreamed into the world of education, work, and recreation.

If we are honest with ourselves, we will admit that our whole structure of relations is rattling and creaking, as people of many, many groups challenge its usefulness to humanity. The demand for a more humane structure and more humane values echoes across the land. Can those of us concerned with children and their books stand passively by? We say no; let us listen to the challenge and re-examine those books.

Towards Positive Human Values

In an age of great and necessary upheaval, new educational materials—including children's books—must be developed. Failure to do so would be a betrayal of our children, for it would leave them stranded and lost in a changing world, unprepared to relate to that process of change. We propose that children's literature become a means for the conscious promotion of human values that will help lead to greater human liberation. We are advocates of a society which will be free of racism, sexism, ageism, materialism, elitism, handicapism and a host of other negative values. We are advocates of a society in which all human beings have the true, not rhetorical, opportunity to realize their full human potential. We therefore frankly advocate books that will help achieve such a society and help prepare children for such a society.

We have named a number of "isms" as our targets. It is important that we offer a definition of each, and some reasons why we feel they must be combatted. (These definitions amplify those given on pp. 4-6.)

Racism is the systematic oppression and exploitation of human beings on the basis of their belonging to a particular racial group or people. Systematic indicates that we must look at the status of the group as a whole, and not at those few individuals who may have climbed a "ladder of success" in the white society. The word *systematic* also connotes practices and policies which are pervasive, regardless of whether they are intentional or unintentional. Racism is different from individual prejudice because it requires the possession of genuine power in a society. It is often used by those with power to divide white people from people of color. As the U.S. Civil Rights Commission stated in 1970, "Racism is any attitude, action or institutional structure which subordinates a person or group because of their color." Thus, racism is no accident, it is not an individual quirk. In the United States, racism is institutionalized and it is white. It is white because the institutions are controlled by white society. So racism is not merely prejudice, but prejudice plus power.

In saying this, we note that the concept of race or racial group is no longer considered scientific. The classification of human beings by races like *caucasian, mongoloid, negroid,* has long been rejected. Yet racism is a fact, a reality, and the word will be used as long as the reality exists.

It is the all-too-rare books like the above that help to achieve a more humanistic society.

TERMINOLOGY DEFINED

Many so-called *minority* people dislike being called that, for various reasons—including the subtle deprecation of being a minority. The term *non-white* has racist implications that white is the norm by which all else is defined. Therefore we will often use the term *third world* in the spirit of the times and the new consciousness described earlier. The exact meaning of third world has sometimes been debated; in this book we use it as a common noun to stand for Black, Chicano, Puerto Rican, Native American, and Asian American peoples.

In children's books, racism has many faces. In the days of *Doctor Dolittle,* it was overt to the point of being grotesque. Today, it may still be overt but it is more often covert, and therefore it becomes a complex problem. In recent years, there has been a growing awareness of racism in children's books as

Both racist illustrations on this page are from Pamela Travers' *Mary Poppins* books. Though many of Travers' books are racist, they nevertheless still appear on many a "recommended reading" list.

a result of the popular pressure mentioned earlier. This has led to the publication of a number of children's books dealing with race relations or with national minority groups. This is good in itself, but all too often these books have been written from a white perspective and are covertly racist. Many readers may at first be misled by an author's "good intentions." Reviewers may hail a new book as liberal, progressive, full of "brotherhood," when in fact it is as racist as ever but in ways that are less obvious (at least to most reviewers, especially those who do not come from the racial group depicted in the book).

Racism in children's books runs from simple omission of third world peoples to stereotypes, white paternalism, and a wide range of other problems. Some types of racist treatment apply to all groups, such as insensitivity to—or abuse of—their language. Some types of racism are particular to one group. For example, while Native Americans may be constantly portrayed as bloodthirsty savages, the problem for Asian Americans is the stereotype of docility and the absence of emotion.

Over the years the Council has studied the different forms racism takes in children's books. Our first major re-evaluation of a children's classic for racist content was done in 1967 by a librarian, Isabelle Suhl, who took on none less than *Doctor Dolittle*. She concluded that the doctor, beloved so long by so many, was in fact the personification of the paternalistic, racist *Great White Father Nobly Bearing the White Man's Burden*. The consternation caused by this article was expressed in editorials across the nation. Even across the seas the London *Times* was appalled at this irreverence. Many more white people today can recognize racism, because of heightened awareness in recent years. But there are more subtle versions of the *Great White Father*—or *Mother*—in contemporary children's books. *Josie's Handful of Quietness* by Nancy C. Smith shows how a friendly white man "adopts" a Chicano migrant family and changes their lives so nicely for the better. The implication is that "non-whites" cannot do it alone; they would be lost without *Great White Father*. Many books about urban Black or Puerto Rican youth have a standard character, the kindly social worker, teacher, or parole officer, who saves the third world child from hopeless delinquency. This character is invariably white.

OMISSION

We find so many different patterns of racism in children's books that only a few more can be mentioned here. There is, first, the book with no third world characters at all, or perhaps only one, when it would be natural to include them—as in almost any urban situation in the United States. This is the racism of total omission; third worlders are invisible, or next-to-invisible, when in fact they are *there*. Such unjustifiable omission tends to support ethnocentricity in the white reader, as well as to promote the idea that racial minorities are tolerable so long as they come only in small quantities (or not at all). For both white and third world readers, the message comes across unmistakably: *WHITE IS THE NORM*. Or, in the words of that little ditty from the streets: "If you're white, all right—if you're brown, get down—if you're black, get back."

Then there are children's books with mixed characters, or primarily third world characters. In general, the existence of racism in the characters' lives is not acknowledged; it would seem that racism just doesn't exist. Problems are purely personal. A racist act may be presented but the author neglects to comment on it—which serves as implicit sanction of the act, leaving the young reader with the impression that it was correct. A third world character may be shown as distrustful of whites, angry, bitter—but the author never explains where those feelings come from. For the reader, the characters are just people "with a chip on their shoulders."

By ignoring the reality of racism and its economic origins, such books are deceitful and do nothing to prepare children of any color for the society around them. In the third world child they encourage confusion and self-hatred and, in the white child, they encourage white chauvinism and distortion of reality. Such books reflect an unwillingness to face the truth about U.S. society and about the responsibility of whites, who hold power and are accountable for racism. At most, racism becomes an unpleasant, minor aberration, rather than a central pivot of this society which affects everyone living in it.

COLOR-BLIND

Lately, there have been an increasing number of books which attempt to deal directly with the problem of racism. Unfortunately, their perspective is almost always white-oriented. The white child learns to accept the Black as "just like me." *The Cay* by Theodore Taylor, which won a host of "brotherhood" awards is a classic example of this. So is *Bright April,* another "favorite." In both, the Black person is finally accepted *by* whites. But what about a Black person's acceptance *of* the white? That is just automatically assumed. This aspect of the relationship has no importance; white is the norm, the standard that counts.

And on what basis has the Black been accepted? Always, it is on the basis of some version of that good old formula; be neat and clean, don't get bitter, patiently turn the other cheek, be intelligent, but don't forget "your place." That formula, in turn, rests on an ideology that is racist to the core. It blames the victims of racism for their long history of oppression. If it is up to the third world people to win "acceptance," then by implication they are defective until they prove themselves worthy of white approval. Also, that ideology includes what has been called "the Bootstrap Syndrome"—or the admonition "Work yourself up the ladder of success. Others have." It is the notion that personal, individual virtue brings inevitable rewards, and that the problems one encounters by being Black will be resolved by the same society that has made blackness a liability. (In other words, that the oppressor out of sheer good will is going to free the oppressed, or the burglar return stolen goods out of compassion for those robbed.) Actual experience of this society simply does not bear out those assumptions. Personal virtue or strength may have worked for many white people, but not for the vast majority of people who are not white—not for any third world people *as a group*.

The whole formula is fraudulent, and to foist it on children is truly abusive. Unfortunately, many readers tend to love the "acceptance" book, because it leaves them all warm and tingly with feelings of, "See, there doesn't have to be hate, does there?" But the problem is not simply hate, which of course nobody wants; it is racism, it is a system. Here again we see the unwillingness to come to grips with the truth about U.S. society and about white responsibility for racism. Racism will never be eliminated by denial of its existence, or by individual solutions instead of social solutions. The problem will not go away by simply saying, "Underneath, we're all the same."

That we're-all-the-same approach is insulting to other racial groups, to their cultures, to their histories, to their languages. The peoples of the United States are not *all* the same, nor do they want to be, nor is equality *sameness*.

OTHER PROBLEMS

Many children's books have been published lately that seem to approve of differences and to view a multicultural society as desirable. Many of these have

The Cay, like many other prize-winning, popular books, demeans the self-image of young Black readers and makes whites feel they have a right to bestow "acceptance" on people of color.

been worthwhile, but many include another set of problems, such as gestures to language differences. The author has the characters speaking English in what the author thinks are constructions of the character's mother tongue ("I go now"). Or the author sprinkles the text with bits of the mother tongue which are full of error. Chicanos and Puerto Ricans speak broken *Engleesh* and Native Americans *How!* their way through life. The richness of Black dialect reflected in June Jordan's *His Own Where* or in John Steptoe's *Stevie* rarely comes across in books by whites, and any gestures white writers make toward its unique qualities usually end up making it sound inferior—which is, of course, the final impression given by all those other gestures—inferiority.

Many other problems come to mind. Asian American children are constantly shown in stories where the highlight is the Lunar New Year celebration (it's "colorful"), when this makes as little sense to them as if most stories about white children focussed on a Fourth of July celebration. Often certain foods are used to make the third world characters seem authentic, but in effect leaving the impression that this is all they eat (tortillas and beans, for example). Supposed cultural patterns are milked for authenticity to the point where one expects that every white child in the United States must think, for example, that every Black family has a dominating mother and a weak father. All in all, when the existence of differences is portrayed as acceptable, those differences often appear in distorted form. They are caricatures, not portraits, and they can do grave damage to the reader.

Too many books about Chinese Americans feature colorful dragons at the Chinese New Year festival. Such repetitious stories are stereotypic, limiting Asian American's full humanity and categorizing them as exotica in the minds of many whites.

Books that endeavor to deal with the historical experiences of racial minorities also have their serious weaknesses. *The Slave Dancer* by Paula Fox tried to show the horrors of slavery and the slave trade, but was nevertheless filled with its own racism. The slaves had no individuality, no spirit, no brains. They were compared at one point to "scrambling rats." The book placed the blame for slavery primarily on Africans themselves—plus a few evil whites— while the U.S. system emerged generally blameless. *The Slave Dancer,* given the American Library Association's (ALA) Newbery Medal for the "most distinguished" work of 1973, may show the horrors of the slave trade, but it did so in such a way that no young reader was left with respect for Black people. The book's main characters expressed hatred and disgust toward Blacks; there was *no* contradiction of their attitudes; so those were the emotions that received validity. At a Council presentation following the ALA award, Black author Sharon Bell Mathis asked the librarians, "If your children were Black, would you give them *The Slave Dancer* to read?"

The lack of full humanity mentioned above pervades many of the children's books with third world characters. Stereotypes are one form of the problem; lack of individualized, realistic human characteristics is just as important. Asian Americans in particular have been the victims of both. They emerge either as Charlie Chan types, laundry-workers, cooks or very studious students (the stereotype) or, as in *The Five Chinese Brothers,* indistinguishable from one another and from all the other Chinese characters in the books, all with the same slant eyes, hair in pigtails, and nauseous yellow coloring. (Has anyone ever seen those storybook-illustration yellows in reality?)

GOOD INTENTIONS DON'T COUNT

The source of the problems described here is racism itself. Most of the books were written by authors who are not from the racial group represented, and who are unable to identify with the group depicted. Furthermore, editors in publishing companies are almost exclusively white and middle class and live in suburbs or in the cities far from the realities of ghetto existence. Centuries of racism on this continent have left book writing and publishing primarily in the hands of a white, Anglo-Saxon, Protestant elite. Centuries of racism have left an ethnocentric majority with little knowledge or understanding of other peoples. No matter how good the *intent* of white authors and artists, they have rarely done a satisfactory job of depicting third world people in children's books.

And it is the final *product* that counts—not the intent. We must be concerned above all with the effects of a book on the children who read it. What happens to children from the racial group depicted when they look in that mirror and see sameness, ugliness, dependency on whites, lack of resistance, acceptance only on the basis of an endless willingness to suffer? What happens when they see something they can never have—whiteness—embodied with superiority and desirability? What happens when they see a pretty world free of racism, which they know to be unreal? What happens when they see their own people always "in trouble with the law"? What happens when they see none of their own people showing strength? What happens when they see their culture and language reduced to quaintness, at best, and more often to inferiority?

There is a similar list of questions for white children, and it also points to a pattern of harmful effects. What happens when white children look in that mirror and see only themselves, although the world itself is not thus? What happens when they see racism go uncondemned? What happens when they see minority people incapable of doing for themselves, desiring only to be accepted by persons unlike themselves? Does this prepare white children for reality? Does it enrich their lives and minds? Does it inspire the best human values, anger against injustice, a desire to unite with others in order to make this a healthy society? Or does it help breed another generation of white chauvinists?

Lawrence Yep's book, below, unlike that on the opposite page, is culturally authentic and makes its Chinese American protagonists complex, fully human characters. Books like this can be recommended for all children.

LOOKING AHEAD

We know that we are asking a lot of children's books. We are asking that third world people be shown as human individuals with a full range of traits and emotions—and at the same time, that their historical group experience be recognized and treated with honesty. We are asking that cultural differences be portrayed—and, at the same time, that those differences be non-stereotyped. We are asking that oppression and suffering be shown—and at the same time, that third world peoples be depicted not only as suffering but also as resisting.

We would even ask that books show the ways in which racism oppresses and exploits white people. Racism dehumanizes its advocates, although few may see it that way at first. Also, there are whites among the dominated of this society, whom the dominators keep in line by the use of racism—telling them to enjoy their superior position because at least they are white; to refrain from joining in common concerns with others who are not white.

It is a lot to ask, and it is very little. Thousands of racist children's books have done untold damage in a wide variety of ways. We have a responsibility to study each of these ways, a responsibility to demand an end to all these ways. It can be done; that has been proven. Some worthwhile children's books about third world peoples have been published. Some excellent books which increase white sensitivity and understanding have been written. To them, we give our unequivocal support. Many have strong points and some weaknesses. Many others have been published which might be called neutral. They do no particular harm. However, we question whether the correct word is "neutral." In the end, a failure to work for change actually supports the status quo. Books can strike a blow against racism. At this point in history, directly or indirectly, one serves either the racist past or a humanistic future.

SEXISM

Although there are similarities, the definition of sexism is more complex than that of racism because its *direct* victims can be found on "both sides"—meaning both women and men. We see the primary victims of sexism as women because they are subordinated in an institutionalized way, as well as by cultural forces. The sexist oppression of men comes mainly, though not exclusively, from cultural forces.

We can therefore define sexism primarily as the systematic oppression and exploitation of human beings on the basis of their belonging to the female sex. Secondarily, we see sexism as the repression of people based on cultural assumptions and definitions of *femininity* and *masculinity,* which prevents both sexes from realizing their full human potential. Briefly, as we have already stated in "Terminology and Definitions," sexism is any attitude, action or institutional practice which subordinates or limits a person on the basis of sex.

As with racism, the possession of power is key. Most real power in the United States lies in the hands of men (although certainly not *all* men). Men use that power to oppress and exploit women. But women *as a group* are without a power base—they have no institutional control by use of which they oppress and exploit men, either as a group or separately (although individual women may exploit individual men, like the rich woman her chauffeur).

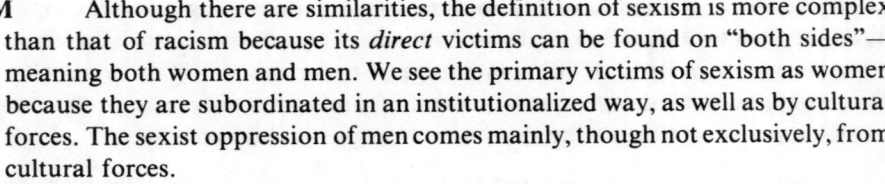

WHO BENEFITS?

Almost all fairy tales, as *Hansel and Gretel* above, stereotype girls as weak, helpless, foolish or passive. The male solves the problem or saves the lovely princess. Modern versions of fairy tales are macho comics, with mainly male super-heros.

The subordination of women is as fundamental to U.S. society as is racism. To limit women to the dual role of housewife and mother serves basic economic purposes; for example, it provides vast amounts of unpaid labor that have been estimated as worth over $20,000 a year per woman. Outside the home, unequal pay for equal work saves business billions of dollars every year (it is estimated that women earn 58 percent of what men earn for similar work). If nursing were a high status occupation, most nurses would be well-paid *men*. But by making this "women's work," a lower salary is justified.

The image of women as an inferior group serves many purposes. Men of all colors can have someone to look down upon, to exploit—which pacifies and deflects their anger away from poverty, injustice and racism. The conservation of life is generally viewed as a *feminine* (read, *inferior*) function. This places peace-keeping and environmental concerns on a scale below *masculine* war-making and profit-making concerns. Definitions of supposed *manhood* and *womanhood* also interlock with the social structure. *Masculinity* is defined in terms of "toughness" and "rugged individuality," while *femininity* is equated with "weakness" and "easily influenced." This kind of *masculinity* often pervades our institutions and foreign policy practices (let's not act *like women* is the unspoken message).

Of course, the male is not seen as superior—not even as competent—in functions such as raising children or "home-making," in activities involving delicate handwork, or in demonstrating tenderness. The female may even be exalted in those roles. But this is hardly an asset. First of all, women are stereotyped as possessing supposedly natural excellence in those functions when it may not be natural at all to many women. Secondly, such functions are rarely, if ever, viewed as commanding the highest respect of the society. They are nice, even necessary, but taken for granted and hardly exciting. They demonstrate no special accomplishment, since they come "naturally." Men are the *real* doers.

SEXISM PLUS

These facts and attitudes have been widely exposed by the women's movement. Not so well understood is the role of sexism in the lives of poor and third world peoples. Women of those groups are, of course, not simply oppressed by sexism, but also by their class status and by racism as well. Furthermore, if white women suffer the stereotypes mentioned above, Chicanas and Puerto Rican women suffer them doubly. Latino women in general are seen as super-passive, super-domestic, and super-submissive to their men. Black women, on the other hand, are often seen as domineering, matriarchal figures. The strong Latino woman who has challenged the welfare office or a racist school system, the Black woman who has stood firmly in support of her husband—these are lost in a neglect or indifference to reality created by stereotypes. Racism and poverty have made sexism worse than ever for the third world woman.

Also not well understood are the ways in which sexism oppresses and limits options for males. There is the male who would rather be a dancer than a football player; who prefers a supportive rather than an aggressive role; who has so-called *feminine* qualities. The pressures put on males to be *real men* in order to avoid ridicule are enormous, and often lead to unhappiness, to lonesomeness, to premature heart attacks, and to death.

How do children's books reflect all this, and what are they doing to correct it—or to sustain it?

As with racial minorities, females are traditionally less present in children's books than males. (Since they compose at least half the population, there is even less excuse.) The concept of white as the norm is matched by the concept of male as the center of attention and female as "the other one." In most books, females who are brave or aggressive or adventurous have been compared to males, just as third world persons get compared—directly or indirectly—to whites. A female who accomplishes a difficult feat is described as remarkable; normally, the author implies, she is just a cheerleader for the male. Normally, it is the boy who saves the day and leads the way; it is the boy who knows the secret way of opening a locked door; it is the boy who calms down his emotional sister. The familiar face of paternalism looms again.

Sexist stereotypes prevail in children's books, and not even the animal world escapes. The little animals in the extraordinarily popular Richard Scarry books may be adorable, but they have exactly the same sexist role-playing that a human family might have. Mr. Bunny do housework? Forget it! Molly Patch's male animal friends cook for her? Never!

Nowadays, this pattern is changing, due to pressure from femininists. However, bookracks in supermarkets and chain stores—where most children's books are sold—do not reflect much change.

LANGUAGE

The language problem is perhaps even greater in the case of sexism than racism, because sexism has a longer history. If *blackness* is equated with *badness* in racist writing, womanhood simply disappears in sexist writing. *He, man, mankind* or *the average man*—supposedly representing both female and male—occur constantly. There are dozens of words with built-in sexism which turn up in children's books, such as *salesman, repairman, mailman, spokesman, manpower,* and *brotherhood* (with "ooh, it's a lady doctor" as counterpart). Women are constantly made into human baggage, as in "man and wife" or "Daddy took the family along to California." The assumption of femaleness or maleness according to role is still another example of sexist language: "Each citizen must pay *his* taxes" or "A good nurse cares about *her* patients' feelings."

FEMALE ROLES

Typical of Latino mothers stereotyped in children's books is this illustration from *Magdalena*, by Louise R. Shotwell and Lilian Obligado.

Ben Shecter's *Molly Patch* not only cooks endlessly for a group of nice male animals, she also nurses their health and their egos. The only two female animals in the crowd are a silly goose and a squabbling hen.

Sexism hasn't resulted in many books with *no* female characters at all, but this is only because of another sexist concept. To leave out the mother would put the father in uncomfortable "female" roles (while a family without a father would have the woman assuming "male" responsibilities). Therefore two women—mom and sis—usually make it into children's books. But they might as well be invisible because they only play roles: baking a pie, setting their hair, welcoming Daddy home from work. For these roles, females even have a uniform: the dress, and an apron over it for mother.

And what about those "girl stories"—meaning books in which the central character is female? Publishers have long claimed that books about girls are less profitable because boys will not read them—while girls will read about boys. "Girl stories" are dull, it seems, which is of course inevitable so long as authors portray girls doing dull things. Recent studies give the lie to the publisher's old-time claim. When stories are written with lively girl characters, just as many boys as girls read them. Examples are *Pippi Longstocking* and *Harriet the Spy*. (The old publishing ratio, used by the industry for years, was three boy characters to one girl character.)

Pippi Longstocking in the South Seas is an anti-sexist book which is racist. (The spunky white girl guides foolish grownup Blacks.) *Boss Cat* below, is a non-racist book which is sexist. (Theme is mother's terror of mice.)

IMPROVEMENT

Lately there have been books with females doing more interesting things. There have even been *anti*-sexist books. One reason appears to be that more women than men write children's books, ironically a function allowed them by sexism itself. (It is not a well-paying profession.)

This is not to say that women cannot write sexist books; many do. And many of the new stories are *semi*-sexist. In *Cissy's Texas Pride,* by Edna Smith Makerney, the central character is an eleven-year-old girl who rides horses well and has great initiative. But her long-range goals are sexist (to get married and be "as pretty and sweet as her mother"). Her mother is the traditional commuter between kitchen and beauty salon. This is a pattern in many of the new books; young females are portrayed untraditionally, but adults are not.

We are not against homemaking or anti-housewife; let that be clear. We only oppose sexist attitudes toward those forms of work. We oppose the idea that housekeeping is the primary, correct and "natural" task of *all* women, and not of *any* men. Our concern is also the notion that housework has less value and importance than work outside the home. We do not oppose women doing housework in children's books so long as they do other things too; so long as men also do housework; and so long as the book does not telegraph a lower value for housework compared to other work.

Many *anti*-sexist books have been published lately about female historical figures from the suffrage movement and other struggles. They fill a giant gap and are much needed in the battle against sexism. Marjorie Drake's *A Question of Courage* and John Anthony Scott's excellent *Fanny Kemble's America* are two examples. The first, however, occasionally points toward materialistic values and elitism. This is a common problem; the book that combats sexism but falls into another "ism"—often racism. In the still popular Newbery Medal winner, *The Matchlock Gun* by Walter D. Edmonds, the "valiant" mother lures three "evil Indians" to their deaths by one blast of a gun. The book includes pages of lurid, racist depictions of Native Americans. Unfortunately, we often find anti-sexist books which are racist—*Pippi (Longstocking) in the South Seas* is another example. And we also find anti-racist books which are sexist.

MALE ROLES

In some books, the story itself may help to combat sexist values. Sexism has labelled women as *emotional* and men as *rational,* and this implies it's bad to get emotional or all hung up with personal problems. By giving importance to feelings and to a humanistic resolution of conflicts, books can have an anti-sexist effect.

Thus far, only a few new books, such as *William's Doll* by Charlotte Zolotow, have explored the role-revision for males as well as females. Because of sexism, having boys do "girl things" is far more controversial than having girls do "boy things." Most of the new anti-sexist books have therefore concentrated on providing more positive, active images of girls. We see this as worthwhile, but the ways in which sexism oppresses the male ought to be dealt with more.

THIRD WORLD FEMALES

The most neglected and stereotyped kinds of females have been women and girls from third world groups. A study made by the Council of 100 books about Puerto Ricans revealed not only the predictable racism but heavy sexism as well. With only a few, minor exceptions, the books mirror those super-traditional stereotypes described earlier. The girls play with dolls, rarely go outside the home alone, learn to speak English, and are generally "sweet." Mothers are grown-up versions of the same, and fathers are supreme commanders. All this does not add up to the general Puerto Rican reality, nor does it do anything positive for Puerto Rican girls reading such books. A Council study of 200 children's books about Chicanos found similar stereotypes.

A 1976 Council study of 80 books about Asian Americans also found sexism, racism, and elitism in constant combination. The sweet, passive females were all ultra genteel—as befits well-mannered stereotypic "Orientals."

Sexism in today's books is far from dead, despite the women's movement; Miss Goody-Goody minces on, with her hair tied in the same pink bow. Even in the current efforts to combat sexism, there is reason for serious dissatisfaction. Too often, books which are anti-sexist are still strictly middle class, still ageist, and often stress competition. On the whole, the new feminist books still do not deal with changing society in any deep or meaningful way. We need books about girls who are not afraid of snakes, but we need more than that. Only the surface of sexism—its cultural form—has been seriously confronted. Its institutionalized foundations, and its links with other aspects of oppression in society, remain untouched.

Rosa-Too-Little, by Sue Felt, depicts the sweet, passive, little Puerto Rican girl.

AGEISM

Ageism is the systematic subordination of human beings on the basis of their age, primarily old age. It is any action or attitude that demeans and/or ridicules old people, that limits the fulfillment of their human potential. Ageism is institutionalized and is also cultural. Forced retirement, lack of adequate government programs to benefit older people, their relegation to atrocious "rest homes"—these institutional abuses work hand in hand with the "Rocking Chair Syndrome" of attitudes toward older people as useless, unproductive nuisances.

Children's books contain a host of stereotypes reflecting that syndrome. In physical appearance, older people are constantly shown with bent bodies, blank faces, dressed in baggy and frumpy clothes, with canes, or endlessly rocking in that chair. Older women are portrayed as sexless; older men as perhaps raunchy in speech but impotent in actuality.

Older people hobble through children's books, loaded down with all sorts of infirmities: deafness, poor sight, forgetfulness. Their speech is "high-pitched" or "halting." Their manners and attitudes are rigid, stubborn, old-fashioned,

Ageism in Children's Books

annoying, interfering—and are often ridiculed. The elders are allowed a minimum of ideas, which they constantly repeat. Sometimes they are allowed to be "wise," but this supposed wisdom is usually given the form of a few truisms or cliches.

Some children's books, such as *A Little at a Time* by David A. Adler and *Mandy's Grandmother* by Liesel M. Skorpen, do present older people as interesting, alive individuals with their own emotional complexity and the ability to interact with younger people as equals. But we still find far too many Grannies clucking "a stitch in time saves nine"; far too many Grandpas forgetting where they put their glasses; far too many older folks who "just can't understand this younger generation."

ANTI-YOUTH

Grandfather, in *A Little at a Time,* is an interesting companion to his grandaughter.

Though we define ageism as oppression of older people, oppression because of age also applies to the young: "You're too young to understand"; "too young to vote"; "too young to go to the store alone." Intelligence and the ability to act responsibly are judged by the sole criterion of physical age, as in the case of older people.

It might at first seem that this form of put-down is not common in children's books, since they are written specifically to appeal to the young. But at a deeper level we see that most children's books are indirectly biased against young people. To say, as many have said, that children's books should not deal with controversial social issues is highly paternalistic. It demeans young people and their interests, their ability to comprehend, their concern with the world beyond their own immediate lives. Children of four and five are developing their self-concepts. They are looking in books to see how the world sees them. They are also exploring in books to see how they are to look at others, to see how concerned they should be about others. Their curiosity deserves respect, just as the intellectual curiosity of an eleven- or twelve-year-old deserves respectful challenges rather than mushy pablum. Limiting the achievement of any child's full human potential is the most anti-human deed of all. It is this anti-human value that permits all the other anti-human values to prevail in children's books.

CLASSISM, ELITISM, AND OTHER "ISMS"

One of the great myths of U.S. society has been that we have no class problem or class conflict. We have a democracy, and anybody who works hard enough can "make it" regardless of whether that person was born rich or poor, white or third world, male or female, etc. If some people do possess more than others, they earned it by working hard. Or they were lucky. But nobody is stuck in a "class."

That myth is being exploded in the minds of more and more people. Failure of the "War Against Poverty" has shown that this country's large percentage of poor remain poor. And the small percentage of very rich remain a small percentage and remain very rich. The realization is growing that this nation really has an elite possessing tremendous power as well as wealth. Ours is, in fact, a class society as well as a society divided by race and sex status.

MATERIALISM

More and more people have also questioned the values that go with our society. Is the definition of success, status, or "a good life" defined primarily in terms of material possessions? Do a second car and a color-cable TV, a golf club membership, and a vacation in the Caribbean really create superiority and self-worth? Should we, it has been asked, judge the moral timber and intelligence of people by such standards? Or could it be that such criteria have been laid down by a system which must sell-sell-sell in order to survive?

ME-FIRST-ISM vs INDIVIDUALITY

Many people have questioned the concept of achieving "a good life" for oneself—at the expense of others and at the expense of principles. They have questioned the concept that says, "If you just work hard, be smarter than the next person, and don't mind stepping on others, you'll climb the ladder of success." From kindergarten to the grave, in school, in sports, on the job, everywhere we are told to compete with other human beings. The football coach stands in the locker-room, symbolizing a whole set of values as he exhorts: "Get out there and WIN, WIN, WIN! Kill 'em if you have to, but WIN!" Competitiveness is a cornerstone of any society that pits people against each other to acquire material possessions.

Competitiveness is an extreme form of another basic value in the society—individualism or me-first-ism. Individualism is the cult of human separateness, the doctrine that each person is indeed "an island." It encourages a dog-eat-dog society, where "I'm looking out for number one," is the prevailing motto. Individual welfare, rather than the group welfare, becomes the goal. It differs from individual*ity,* which is simply the special personality qualities of each human being. No two people—or trees or animals or any living things—are exactly alike. These differences are good; they enrich human relations and society. Individual*ity* is a reality; it cannot be denied and should be encouraged. But individual*ism* is a philosophy of life; it has not always existed in every human society and should be discouraged as a highly negative force. Sometimes, of course, the line between the two is blurred. Some so-called individual*ity* is actually the result of negative conditioning, and it is anti-social. The key question must be: does a particular quality in a person oppress others? Does it serve that person alone, or humanity as a whole? Since our educational system, and our culture as a whole, encourage elitism, materialism, and competitiveness (including me-first-ism), it is inevitable that we find these values in children's books as well.

If our society did truly encourage individuality, it would have made the fulfillment of individual potential a real possibility for everyone—whether male or female, white or third world, rich or poor, young or old, non-disabled or disabled.

Children's books also reinforce the notion that there are only individual problems in this society—no class problems. If you can save yourself, then all's right with the world. In *A Bicycle from Bridgetown,* by Dawn C. Thomas, a poor boy finds an old, lost bicycle and is rewarded for his honesty, by the owner, with a brand new bike. This takes place in Barbados, of all places, where the poor but happy "natives" just watch the tourists come and go, fascinated by their clothes and other goodies. The author makes no comment on the brutal contrast between rich tourists and poor "natives," thus giving tacit support to the status quo. Seen through the author's eyes, it is material possessions—starting with the bicycle—that determine everyone's relationships, and the assumption is that those relations are as they should be. Edgar has a bicycle at the end of the book; thus we can forget about the rest of his class and his people. Perhaps they are all supposed to rise in the world by finding lost things and returning them. The author must want children to assume this is possible; we deny this is a valid assumption.

We realize that the author's intentions might be good—to encourage individual strength, self-reliance, honesty. Unfortunately, the actual results of

such books is to encourage elitism, materialism, me-first-ism. The reality of our society, as said above, is a division into social groups or classes which operates for the benefit of the few at the expense of the many. This must be changed, not endorsed. Such books serve as a matrix of lies and fraudulent solutions.

STATUS AND WORK

Madeena Spray Nolen wrote and Jim La Marche illustrated this rare children's book dealing with unemployment. Very well done.

"Poor but honest" characters used to be common in children's books. They still appear occasionally, but are lost in the tide of middle- and upper-class people whose activities, lifestyle, and problems have little relevance to those below them in the social structure. Factory and blue-collar workers, of any racial group, are the rarest of storybook specimens. Families on welfare do turn up, most usually in books about Blacks. Manual labor is generally viewed as inferior to intellectual or professional work. While a friendly policeperson, mail carrier, or garbage collector may appear, books fail to bring out the fact that manual labor is all-important to society. Children get the message, in obvious or subtle form: some people are better than others because they have supposedly "good" jobs, "good" homes, "good" clothing, "good" taste, "good" manners, "good" speech.

The heroic and exciting stories of labor organizing for decent pay and working conditions are rarely considered reading fare for children. And children are given only the barest notion of what a job entails, of how machines are built, of how they are run, and of how all this impacts on the women and men and families involved. The dignity, or lack of dignity, in work situations is also untouched in children's books. Unless children are taught that all useful work merits respect and a living wage, they will develop into adults who feel they are superior and have a right to look down on others who earn less. Or they will become workers who passively accept low status and low pay. An author's approach to status and work can convey elitism or egalitarianism. Sadly, children's books convey the former.

ESCAPISM AND CONFORMISM

Escapism and conformism are siblings. They belong to the same family as elitism, materialism, competitiveness.

Many children's books encourage the reader to wait for luck, magic, or help from some rich or powerful person in order to solve problems. The aforementioned *A Bicycle from Bridgetown* exemplifies this tendency, as do most fairy tales. They may postulate morality, as the prerequisite for that luck, magic, or help, but this does not undo the basic escapism of such stories. One can be honest fifteen times over without it ever bringing a new bicycle; the solution offered is not really one's own initiative or morality, but the entrance on the scene of that outside force.

In rejecting escapism—defined as an evasion of unpleasant reality—we do not propose an end to fantasy in children's books. Good fantasy can be a splendid stimulus to the imagination. But when a book encourages escape into the fantastic as a *substitute* for confronting reality, it does the reader no good at all. It discourages children from examining problems realistically and then acting. It makes children feel that they are helpless pawns in the game of life, rather than that they can indeed fight for their beliefs, their rights, and a better society for all.

DON'T MAKE WAVES

Conformism trails along behind escapism, implying that the best behavior is to leave the boat unrocked. *Marly the Kid* by Susan Pfeffer, a nice book in some ways, ends with the rebellious Marly choosing not to join a group of students who organized to participate in her challenge of the school system. She conforms, after all. (As a substitute, Marly decides to become the first overweight cheerleader at her school—an example of an individual, rather than a collective, action.)

Conformism discourages readers from questioning whether the "usual" way of doing things is best for all people concerned. It serves to prop up the status quo. In saying this, we do not advocate an end to norms as such, or to behavioral rules; we do not advocate a denial of all standards, a total absence of order—anarchy. We urge that existing norms be re-examined in the light of new consciousness and in the light of what is truly best for most people. We are, in fact, highly concerned with norms; the need is for new ones, *not* the elimination of norms. Non-conformism with the worst in this society should mean conformism with the best.

HANDICAPISM

We have defined handicapism as the subordination of people because of a physical or mental disability. So many children's "classics" have featured cruel villains who are minus a hand, a leg, or an eye that disability itself has become a way of connoting evil. Many books offer "comical" scenes with a deaf person, a stutterer, or an overweight woman. Disabled people are pictured as pathetic (Tiny Tim in *A Christmas Carol*), as sinister (Long John Silver in *Treasure Island*), or are presented as interesting solely because of their disability—making them less than fully human. Children have been given a grossly distorted image of people with disabilities and we believe the only way to right the harm done is to call for affirmative action in portraying people with disabilities in new children's books. The rights of disabled people to work, to decent pay, to transportation, to education and to a full social life are rights that children's books should make young people aware of—and concerned about.

The book below, about a girl with impaired sight, is recommended for adolescents.

LITERARY AND ARTISTIC QUALITY

At this point, one may cry for a halt to all the "isms" and demand some words about *quality* in children's books. After all, children deserve beautiful writing and art; they are values, too. Not only content, but also form, is important.

We could not agree more warmly, and the guidelines we present call for evaluating children's books for form as well as content. Good values in no way justify a poorly written book. Books that are stylistically admirable but that transmit anti-human values causing children harm and pain cannot be justified either. With such books, one can hardly talk about their "beauty"; the inner ugliness of their racism or sexism, ageism, or handicapism, corrupts the very word itself. This type of book is especially venal because, by the very skill of its writing or art work, it is likely to impress a child more. The more exciting, the more compelling, the more realistic it seems, the more damage it can do; its smooth surface masks its true nature all the more effectively.

There is no automatic correlation between good values and good writing, or bad values and bad writing. Nor is there contradiction between good values and good writing, bad values and bad writing. We seek both good values and good writing. Authors and artists who wish to combat anti-human values in children's books have a responsibility to offer the best quality in their work as well. If we have emphasized content more than form, it is because good form has traditionally been in demand but good content has not. Stylistic values are already recognized; human values are not—at this time. And these are the times that concern us.

To those who argue that it is not the business of children's books to be the vehicle of change, we answer with our opening statement: no writer is just a reporter. All books contain messages and, by tolerating them, we are in effect endorsing those messages. This we cannot do—not when the message is racism or sexism, materialism or ageism, or any other anti-human value.

Books together with television, schools, comics, advertisements, and of course, adult behavior, are the forces that socialize children, mold their ideas. These forces today are almost always sexist, elitist, and materialist. They are often racist, ageist, and handicapist. Far from whimsy—in whose name those forces often appear—they have tenacious societal roots. To combat them requires a constant, difficult, uphill struggle. Along with many other people, we are committed to that struggle for a single reason: we care about the future of our children and of all children.

STORYBOOK RATING INSTRUMENT

The checklist that follows is for evaluating new children's books or for re-evaluating old books. It is worthwhile to repeat the distinction between "*non*-racist" and "*non*-sexist" books as against "*anti*-racist" and "*anti*-sexist" books. There are many books which, for example, are not sexist, but could never be seen as contributing toward the elimination of sexism. An *anti-sexist* book would contribute in some way to the *elimination* of sexism; a *sexist* book contributes to the *maintenance* of sexist oppression; and a *non-sexist* book does neither.

We also consider that building a positive image for a female and/or third world reader is—in our present society—an anti-sexist or anti-racist act, and we define books that achieve such an objective in those terms. Is it also important that white and/or male children perceive those positive images? We answer strongly in the affirmative. We also hope for books calling for another value only previously hinted at: "Inspire action against social oppression." To achieve that objective is one step *beyond* anti-racism or anti-sexism. Very, very few books fit in that category, but it is the value we wish to encourage most of all.

Naturally there are borderline cases in all the categories, and other complications. No checklist can provide for all the subtleties, all the hidden messages, all the qualities of a book. Reviewers, whether they work as individuals or in teams, must at some point rely on judgments and preferences which are uniquely their own. A subjective element will inevitably enter every analysis.

WHO SHOULD REVIEW BOOKS?

While these guidelines were prepared to assist all parents, librarians, teachers and editors involved in book selection, we suggest a cautionary note. The Council has always followed a policy of involving reviewers who are members of the particular group depicted in any book, and we believe that books about Blacks are best reviewed by Blacks, that books about Chicanos are best reviewed by Chicanos, and books about disabled people reviewed by disabled people, etc. It is extremely difficult for a member of the dominant society to know whether or not a book about a dominated people is culturally authentic or whether or not it is flawed by stereotypes and covert bias. That is why, whenever possible, selection teams for libraries and schools should be strongly pluralistic and include people especially sensitive to third world, feminist, and other social issues.

The guidelines we present are defined by our present understanding of ourselves and our society. Ridicule of third world people and women, or putting down or poking fun at any group may be perfectly acceptable in a future society. But these guidelines are intended for the oppressive society that exists today. So our criteria are not timeless, nor are our targets. They do suit today's situation, in which revised values are certainly blowing in the wind and the times are not only changing but profoundly revolutionary. We make no claim to eternal verities; if anything, we look forward to the day when guidelines like this will no longer be relevant.

Story Book Rating Instrument

	Art	Words		Art	Words		Art	Words
anti-Racist			non-Racist			Racist — omission / commission		
anti-Sexist			non-Sexist			Sexist		
anti-Elitist			non-Elitist			Elitist		
anti-Materialist			non-Materialist			Materialist		
anti-Ageist			non-Ageist			Ageist		
anti-Conformist			non-Conformist			Conformist		
anti-Escapist			non-Escapist			Handicapist		
Builds positive image of females/minorities			Builds negative image of females/minorities				Excellent	Good	Fair	Poor
						Literary quality				
Inspires action vs. oppression			Supports status quo			Art quality				
Stresses Cooperation			Stresses Competition			Culturally authentic				

Racist by omission means that third world people could logically be included but are not.

Racist by commission means that the content or the art is overtly or openly racist in some way.

Non before a negative value means that the book's impact is neutral in that regard and does nothing to challenge the status quo, thereby reinforcing it.

Anti before a negative value means that the book is taking a conscious, deliberate stand to combat that negative value.

Inspires action against oppression means that the book not only describes injustice but in some way encourages readers to act against injustice, preferably to act cooperatively with others.

Ten Quick Ways To Analyze Children's Books For Sexism And Racism

(credit note: The following was developed by the Council, in flyer form, for distribution through organizational mailings and for other purposes. More than 200,000 copies of the flyer have been distributed. See p. 104.)

Both in school and out, young children are exposed to racist and sexist attitudes. These attitudes—expressed over and over in books and in other media—gradually distort their perceptions until stereotypes and myths about minorities and women are accepted as reality. It is difficult for a librarian or teacher to convince children to question society's attitudes. But if a child can be shown how to detect racism and sexism in a book, the child can proceed to transfer the perception to wider areas. The following ten guidelines are offered as a starting point in evaluation of children's books from this perspective.

1. CHECK THE ILLUSTRATIONS

Look for Stereotypes. A stereotype is an over-simplified generalization about a particular group, race, or sex, which usually carries derogatory implications. Some infamous (overt) stereotypes of Blacks are the happy-go-lucky, watermelon-eating Sambo and the fat, eye-rolling "mammy"; of Chicanos, the sombrero-wearing peon, or fiesta-loving, macho bandito; of Asian Americans, the inscrutable, slant-eyed "Oriental"; of Native Americans, the naked savage or "primitive" craftsperson and his "squaw"; of Puerto Ricans, the switchblade-toting, teenage gang member; of women, the completely domesticated mother, the demure, doll-loving little girl or the wicked stepmother. While you may not always find stereotypes in the blatant forms described, look for variations which in any way demean or ridicule characters because of their race or sex.

Look for Tokenism. If there are minority characters in the illustrations, do they look just like whites except for being tinted or colored in? Do all minority faces look stereotypically alike, or are they depicted as genuine individuals with distinctive features?

Who's Doing What? Do the illustrations depict minorities in subservient and passive roles or in leadership and action roles? Are males the active "doers" and females the inactive observers?

Females and people of color are grossly stereotyped in all of the very popular *Tintin* series. These are published in 31 countries. Seventeen are published by Little, Brown in the United States.

2. CHECK THE STORY LINE

The liberation movements have led publishers to weed out many insulting passages, particularly from stories with Black themes and from books depicting female characters; however, racist and sexist attitudes still find expression in less obvious ways. The following checklist suggests some of the subtle, covert forms of bias to watch for.

Standard for Success. Does it take "white" behavior standards for a minority person to "get ahead"? Is "making it" in the dominant white society projected as the only ideal? To gain acceptance and approval, do third world persons have to exhibit extraordinary qualities—excel in sports, get A's, etc? In friendships between white and third world children, is it the third world child who does most of the understanding and forgiving?

Resolution of Problems. How are problems presented, conceived, and resolved in the story? Are minority people considered to be "the problem"? Are the oppressions faced by minorities and women represented as casually related to an unjust society? Are the reasons for poverty and oppression explained, or are they accepted as inevitable? Does the story line encourage passive acceptance or active resistance? Is a particular problem that is faced by a minority person resolved through the benevolent intervention of a white person?

Role of Women. Are the achievements of girls and women based on their own initiative and intelligence, or are they due to their good looks or to their relationship with boys? Are sex roles incidental or critical to characterization and plot? Could the same story be told if the sex roles were reversed?

3. LOOK AT THE LIFESTYLES

Are third world persons and their setting depicted in such a way that they contrast unfavorably with the unstated norm of white, middle-class suburbia? If the minority group in question is depicted as "different," are negative value judgments implied? Are minorities depicted exclusively in ghettos, barrios, or migrant camps? If the illustrations and text attempt to depict another culture, do they go beyond over-simplifications and offer genuine insights into another lifestyle? Look for inaccuracy and inappropriateness in the depiction of other cultures. Watch for instances of the "quaint-natives-in-costume" syndrome (most noticeable in areas like clothing and custom, but extending to behavior and personality traits as well).

4. WEIGH THE RELATIONSHIPS BETWEEN PEOPLE

Do the whites in the story possess the power, take the leadership, and make the important decisions? Do minorities and females function in essentially supporting, subservient roles?

How are family relationships depicted? In Black families, is the mother always dominant? In Latino families, are there always lots of children? If the family is separated, are societal conditions—unemployment, poverty—cited among the reasons for the separation?

5. NOTE THE HEROS

For many years, books showed only "safe" minority heros—those who avoided serious conflict with the white establishment of their time. Minority groups today are insisting on the right to define their own heros (of both sexes) based on their own concepts and struggles for justice.

When minority heros do appear, are they admired for the same qualities that have made white heros famous or because what they have done has benefited white people? Ask this question: "Whose interests is a particular hero really serving?" The interests of the hero's own people? Or the interests of white people?

6. CONSIDER THE EFFECTS ON A CHILD'S SELF-IMAGE

Are norms established which limit any child's aspirations and self-concepts? What effect can it have on third world children to be continuously bombarded with images of the color white as the ultimate in beauty, cleanliness, virtue, etc., and the color black as evil, dirty, menacing, etc.? Does the book reinforce or counteract positive associations with the color white and negative associations with the color black?

What happens to a girl's self-image when she reads that boys perform all of the brave and important deeds? What about a girl's self-esteem if she is not "fair" of skin and slim of body?

In a particular story, is there one or more persons with whom a minority child can readily identify to a positive and constructive end?

7. CONSIDER THE AUTHOR'S OR ILLUSTRATOR'S BACKGROUND

Analyze the biographical material on the jacket flap or the back of the book. If a story deals with a minority theme, what qualifies the author or illustrator to deal with the subject? If the author and illustrator are not members of the minority being written about, is there anything in their background that would specifically recommend them as the creators of this book?

8. CHECK OUT THE AUTHOR'S PERSPECTIVE

No author can be entirely objective. All authors write from a cultural as well as from a personal context. Children's books in the past have traditionally come from authors who were white and who were members of the middle class, with one result being that a single ethnocentric perspective has dominated children's literature in the United States. With any book in question, read carefully to determine whether the direction of the author's perspective substantially weakens or strengthens the value of his/her written work. Is the perspective patriarchal or feminist? Is it solely Eurocentric or do third world perspectives also surface?

9. WATCH FOR LOADED WORDS

A word is loaded when it has offensive overtones. Examples of loaded adjectives (usually racist) are "savage," "primitive," "conniving," "lazy," "superstitious," "treacherous," "wily," "crafty," "inscrutable," "docile," and "backward."

Look for sexist language and adjectives that exclude or in any way demean girls or women. Look for use of the male pronoun to refer to both males and females. While the generic use of the word "man" was accepted in the past, its use today is outmoded. The following examples show how sexist language can be avoided: ancestors instead of forefathers; chairperson instead of chairman; community instead of brotherhood; fire-fighters instead of firemen; manufactured instead of manmade; the human family instead of the family of man.

The illustration below, from *Osceola, Seminole Leader* (1976), reinforces racism.

10. LOOK AT THE COPYRIGHT DATE

Books on minority themes—usually hastily conceived—suddenly began appearing in the mid and late 1960's. There followed a growing number of "minority experience" books to meet the new market demand, but these books were still written by white authors, edited by white editors, and published by white publishers. They therefore reflected a white point of view. Not until the early 1970's did the children's book world begin to even remotely reflect the realities of a pluralistic society. The new direction resulted from the emergence of third world authors writing about their own experiences in an oppressive society. This promising direction has been reversing in the late 1970's. Non-sexist books, with rare exceptions, were not published before 1972 to 1974.

The copyright dates, therefore, can be a clue as to how likely the book is to be overtly racist or sexist, although a recent copyright date, of course, is no guarantee of a book's relevance or sensitivity. The copyright date only means the year the book was published. It usually takes two years—and often much more than that—from the time a manuscript is submitted to the publisher to the time it is actually printed and put on the market. This time lag meant very little in the past, but in a period of rapid change and new consciousness, when children's book publishing is attempting to be "relevant," it is becoming increasingly significant.

BIAS IN TEXTBOOKS

Introduction

(credit note: The following section is adapted from an unpublished manuscript entitled Presenting People *authored by the editorial personnel at Scott, Foresman & Company.)*

> There is no such thing as a neutral educational process. Education either functions as an instrument to facilitate the integration of the younger generation into the logic of the present system and bring about conformity to it, or it becomes "the practice of freedom," the means by which men and women deal critically and creatively with reality and discover how to participate in the transformation of their world.
>
> Richard Shaull, Foreword to Paolo Freire's
>
> *Pedagogy of the Oppressed*

Although textbooks compete with the mediating forces of culture, mass media, and noncurricular aspects that influence children, books still remain the authoritative vehicle for prescribing the knowledge and roles which students are expected to assimilate. And assimilate they do! Edward Hall is one of many critics who have observed that children unconsciously absorb the values as well as the subject content of books. He states in *The Silent Language* that because these values have the potential to develop and perpetuate negative self-images in students, each book might carry the warning: "This book may be dangerous; read with caution."

When books present prescribed roles or behavior and limit options according to race, sex, disability or class, they subvert, rather than encourage, the ultimate goal of education—personal growth. Through sexist language a girl may learn that *she* is a *he*. Eurocentric language may teach minority students that *they* are not *we*, and white students that *we* are the norm. But language is only part of the problem. Until very recently, third world children and girls in general found few national heros, storybook characters, and role models with whom they could identify. Even the figure at the top of the evolutionary chart in biology texts has traditionally been a white male.

Although textbooks of recent copyright have begun to acknowledge the existence of a world beyond the white, patriarchal, middle-class, suburban family, they still contain biases, often between the lines and behind the pictures. Such biases, conveying potent messages to those who read books, can take various forms—the inclusion or omission of certain information; a distorted point of view; limited roles assigned to females or males; a secondary status accorded to minority people; the use of racist or sexist language; editorial materials that are themselves biased or that fail to expose the biases in a work. Each of the preceding serves to limit, slant, or in some way control information presented to students. And each serves to restrict students' options according to their class, sex, disability, or racial backgrounds.

Only after such biases are pinpointed and examined can guidelines become an effective tool for detecting and eliminating discrimination in school textbooks. But no guidelines, however explicit, can provide a simple solution to the complexities of bias in books. Combatting biases involves more than the replacement of the generic use of the word *man,* the inclusion of ethnic-sounding names, or the presentation of minority people in illustrations—although these gestures are a beginning. Essential changes involve a reappraisal of materials, a rejection of stereotypical assumptions, a search for fresh sources, ideas, approaches, and viewpoints, and an inclusion of lifestyles, backgrounds, values, and heritages reflecting our diverse, pluralistic society.

In using guidelines to appraise educational materials, the overall effect must always be considered. To accept or reject a book on the basis of one picture, a single story, or an isolated sentence is an unfair evaluation. One must look at the cumulative effect of a book in ascertaining whether or not it offers an authentic, unbiased portrayal of people, roles, cultures, values, and options.

Although the guidelines that follow concentrate primarily on content and the values implied therein, it should be understood that we are in no way deemphasizing the importance of literary, artistic, or educational quality.

Even when every effort is made to eliminate bias from new textbooks, there will still remain literary works, historical documents and copyrighted material that are unquestionably biased. Many of these materials cannot be eliminated—nor should they be—since such elimination would serve to misrepresent history. By teaching students how to recognize bias, and by guiding them to gain insights into its causes, educators can supply students with the critical skills that are necessary to eliminate bias. We recommend the constructive use of biased materials to examine the social, cultural, and economic influences surrounding a literary work or a historical document.

UNDERREPRESENTATION

(credit note: Much of the following section is excerpted from an article by Jeana Wirtenberg, of the National Institute of Education, to be published in the Bulletin *during 1980. See p. 104 for availability.)*

Let's examine statistics about the makeup of the student body in U.S. schools. Females, of course, comprise slightly over 50 per cent of the students. But language arts, math and science texts assuredly do not offer them anything like 50 per cent of the positive role models or the page space offered to males. Nor do history texts do justice—in fact they do serious injustice—to the role of women in our growth and development as a nation, economically and culturally.

About one in every five students is a member of a racial minority group. If present population trends continue, that figure is expected to reach one in every four students in the very near future. While there is greater visibility of darker-skinned people in the newer textbooks, the proportion of characters and perspectives does not begin to approach their proportions in the student population. As with women, the importance of minorities in U.S. cultural and economic growth is undervalued and underrepresented.

One in every ten students is, to some extent, disabled. They, too, are entitled to positive textbook images and have a right to see their special concerns reflected in school materials. Today, more than one of every five children come from a single parent household. Within a few years it will be one of every four. Why do textbooks continue to emphasize the nuclear family in which daddy works while mom and the kids stay at home? Today, only one of every seven children is from such a family. Reality for about half of all students is that their mothers work. (That percentage is rising.) Reality for many students is that their families live below the poverty level. Yet inspection of current textbooks shows a totally misleading picture of the realities of U.S. life.

The serious underrepresentation of minorities and women in widely used textbooks has been amply documented. Gwyneth Britton examined 5,242 stories from 244 different reading textbooks commonly used in 1974 for their treatment of Blacks, Native Americans, Chicanos, Puerto Ricans, Asian Americans, and others. Minority males were not underrepresented in this sample. Minority females, however, about 10 per cent of the population, were only 3 per cent of the main characters. Consequently, the underrepresentation of minorities was entirely due to marked underrepresentation of minority females.

Britton also found that white males were 58 per cent of all characters, and white females 15 per cent. In contrast, white males were about 40 per cent and white females 42 per cent of the U.S. population. So *all* females were *under*represented, and white males were the only ones *over*represented.

Other studies conducted during the 1970's provide corroborative evidence for the overrepresentation of white males and the underrepresentation of both minority and majority females in textbooks. In their 1974 study entitled *Biased Textbooks,* Lenore J. Weitzman and Dianne Rizzo counted the frequency of majority and minority males and females illustrated in the most widely used textbooks, for grades one through six, in five subject areas: reading, spelling, mathematics, science, and social studies. Majority males were 57 per cent of all illustrated characters in the textbooks sampled—again, overrepresented. Minority males were also slightly overrepresented in this study (12 per cent, though only 9 per cent of the population).

Weitzman and Rizzo also found that the proportion of minority and female characters, in each series, *decreased* as the grade level of the textbooks increased. For example, the percentage of minority persons in mathematics textbooks decreased from 25 per cent to 15 per cent and in science books from 11 per cent to 8 per cent from the first to the sixth grade textbooks.

(Findings of studies on specific minority groups, females, and older persons appear in other sections of this book.)

During the 1960's and early 1970's basal readers of most publishers routinely featured three boy stories to one girl story.

IDEAL VS. REAL

To present positive role models for all children, and to reflect the population distribution of our society, textbooks would have to portray 50 per cent females in active leadership positions; 20 per cent minority people; 10 per cent older people; and 10 per cent disabled people. In the real world, of course, non-disabled white males between the ages of 20 and 65 control over 80 per cent of active leadership positions, even though they are roughly 20 per cent of the population. So the dilemma is whether to "tell it like it is" or to present the ideal society we envision.

Both the reality *and* the ideal must appear in textbooks. There actually are some female, minority, older, and disabled people in leadership positions. Such portrayals do not reflect an impossibility; besides, they help to destroy stereotypes and they create much needed role models. On the other hand, we do children a disservice if we instill illusions which leave them ill-prepared for reality when they leave school. Young people should learn of the societal roadblocks that must be surmounted before equity is achieved. They should learn why and how to create the social changes necessary to achieve equity.

The tendency to soft-pedal the unpleasant realities of society in children's texts is understandable. However, we believe that to misrepresent reality fails in the end to help children prepare for full participation in society. The reality of exploitation of some groups by others should be honestly stated and explained. Children should learn, in their texts, the unpleasant truth about race and sex oppression, about national conquest, about poverty and other inequalities. The fact that conflict is the likely result of oppression and inequalities should also be faced squarely.

A word of caution is needed. When dealing with issues of poverty, poor health, inadequate housing and other realities, beware of presenting these as solely the concerns of ethnic and racial minorities within the United States. Two factors need emphasis. First, minority peoples are the victims of historic, social, and economic processes which have resulted in their present circumstances. Second, oppressed minorities continue to struggle and achieve vital, vibrant lives and cultures, despite their socioeconomic conditions.

All of this requires that textbook content must become more respectful of children's capacity to recognize social injustice, and it must display confidence that children can be critical of the way our society operates without losing faith in their country and its future.

Bias In Basal Readers

(credit note: The following section is adapted from an unpublished manuscriph entitled Presenting People *authored by the editorial personnel at Scott, Foresman & Company.)*

Elementary reading texts have traditionally created a simplified world for children, a world that is prescriptive in the attitudes and behavior patterns it establishes, in the roles it presents to males and females of different races, and in the aspects of life it includes or omits. Despite recent efforts to correct past abuses, elementary textbooks are still generally directed to a white, middle-class, patriarchal society. And children are unconsciously assimilating (and will perpetuate) the values and roles prescribed by the textbooks they read.

Though textbook bias today is more subtle than it used to be, books still do not adequately reflect the cultural diversity of our society. Institutional racism and sexism still are not acknowledged; instead social problems are relegated to unrealistic individual solutions—pat answers that in no way address themselves to the societal causes of discrimination. Most of the harsh facts of society have been sugar-coated in an approach that presents the United States as a land of equal opportunity and freedom. When only the best aspects of our society are presented, students will see no need to improve it, no need to overcome its injustices.

The stories in elementary reading textbooks, by and large, fail to encourage young people to investigate ideas, to expand their views, to develop flexible thinking patterns, to make informed judgments. For these skills, males and females of all classes and races must be able to envision themselves in a wide variety of roles, functioning effectively in a realistic world—a world that includes their own experiences and contains recognizable human beings. Such a world includes working mothers, day-care centers, divorce, alternatives to the nuclear family (childless couples, single-parent families), real emotions, defeats, death, family conflict, stepparents who are not villains, disabled people, and problems that are not immediately solved.

In this world are older people who are neither witches nor silly caricatures, families that cope with problems more serious than a lost puppy, and people who display joy, anger, compassion, sadness, love—emotions neglected or treated superficially in many stories.

Sexism In Basal Readers And Other Textbooks, Too

SEXISM IS: any attitude, action, or institutional practice which subordinates people because of their sex or assigns roles in society on the basis of sex.

SEXISM IS EVIDENCED IN U.S. SOCIETY BY: women's earnings, for full time work, being 58 per cent of men's. This percentage is *lower* than it was 20 years ago. Women who have completed college earn *less,* on an average, than men who have completed elementary school. Women are concentrated in a small number of low-paying fields while men hold a virtual monopoly in high-paying fields. Much of women's work, crucial to maintaining society, receives no financial compensation at all—bearing and raising children, maintaining a household, caring for sick family members. Women hold about 5 per cent of public offices in the United States (and even a much smaller percentage of the top posts), and they are less than 2 per cent of top-level business executives.

EDUCATION HELPS MAINTAIN SEXISM BY: socializing children to accept roles, behaviors, and career choices based upon their sex. These roles are constricting to both sexes, but they are especially limiting to the options open to girls.

TEXTBOOKS UNDERREPRESENT FEMALES: studies of **reading textbooks** indicate that boys and men appear as major characters in overwhelmingly larger numbers than girls and women. For example, Terry Saario, Carol Jacklin, and Carol Tittle analyzed four widely-used elementary reading series from different publishers in 1973. Thirty-two per cent of all starring roles centered around females, but 68 per cent around males. Adult males appeared as main characters more than five times as often as did adult females, and male children starred in about twice as many stories as did female children.

A study by Women on Words and Images (WOWI) titled *Dick and Jane as Victims: Sex Stereotyping in Children's Readers,* was published in 1972 and updated in 1975. This study initially examined 2,760 stories appearing in 134 elementary readers from 14 publishers. The 1975 revised study examined readers published between 1972 and 1975 from nine major publishers. There was no improvement over 1972, and the ratio dividing male and female representation actually *increased* from 5:2 in 1972 to 7:2 in 1975.

Mathematics textbooks were studied in 1977 by Barbara Steele who analyzed word problems and pictures of human figures in six popular elementary mathematics series. Female characters appeared in 35 per cent of all illustrations, compared to 65 per cent for male characters. Males were referred to in word problems almost three times as frequently as females.

Henry Kepner and Lilane Koehn examined 24 math texts representing eight major publishers to determine if there was improvement in the portrayal of women from the early to the late 1970's. Males constituted 62 per cent of all illustrated characters, and females 38 per cent. Fifty-nine per cent of all word problems concerned males, and 41 per cent females.

Can you imagine a boy sweeping on a book with this title? This is a 1975 book for hearing-impaired children who are learning American Sign Language.

Kepner and Koehn updated this study by examining three new series published between 1975 and 1977. Now males constituted 58 per cent of illustrated characters, and females 42 per cent. In word problems, however, there was a marked change. The problems in two out of three series showed a larger percentage of females than males, with only one book having males identified more frequently.

Science textbooks were analyzed by Lenore Weitzman and Dianne Rizzo. They found elementary texts the most male-oriented of all. Three out of four pictures in these books were of males. Weitzman and Rizzo concluded: "Throughout the science series the textbooks seem to imply that females have no place in the world of science."

Louis Arnold studied two sets of popular high school earth science curriculums in 1975. Photographs, drawings, and index listings all showed significant bias against women.

Foreign language textbooks were not exempt. Rhoda Stern examined 25 foreign language texts published between 1970 and 1974 for elementary school through college. Stern found numerous dialogues between two men (22 in one book), but almost none between two women (two in the same book). The texts provided many quotations, stories, and photographs of men, but only a few about women. In one book, important men were quoted 30 times, important women twice. In all of the books, there were 38 stories about men, one about a woman. Of a total of 45 photographs and portraits, only five were of women.

Career education textbooks were analyzed by Lois Heshusious-Gilsdorf and Dale Gilsdorf in 1975. Two widely used career education series depicted 25 per cent of all working persons as females, and 75 per cent as males. Women on Words and Images (WOWI) randomly selected 84 sets of materials from more than 600 commercially marketed materials (e.g., textbooks, work books, filmstrips, cassettes). WOWI found that the materials at both the elementary and the secondary levels portrayed males more than twice as often as females.

A study of **U.S. history textbooks** by the Feminist Press was updated in 1979. They examined 12 popular textbooks published since 1974. The average number of pages devoted to women improved from one page, in the earlier study, to 14 pages—out of an average of 700 pages per book! Their report stated:

> Since the texts which we surveyed continue to be organized around political and military events, the history of all oppressed groups—not only that of women—is underrepresented. The objective has been to include these groups within the "mainstream of history," rather than to raise questions about what the "mainstream of history" is. In order to include women's history in texts, a number of questions need to be asked concerning such issues as periodization, definitions of progress, definitions of power. What are the major turning points in history for women? Are they different from those for men? How do these turning points differ for women from different social, racial, and ethnic groups? Are periods traditionally labeled "progressive," progressive for women as well as for men?

This booklet is a study of sexism in high school textbooks on U.S. Government. It is available from KNOW. (See p. 104.)

Once such questions are asked, then texts will be reconceptualized. As long as such reconceptualization of history does not take place and as long as the basic topics needed to explore women's lives remain taboo in high school history texts, then women's past and present will remain inaccessible to students.

(credit note: The first five of the six paragraphs below are adapted from guidelines prepared by the McGraw-Hill Book Company.)

TEXTBOOKS SHOULD: treat men and women primarily as people, not primarily as members of opposite sexes; stress shared humanity and common attributes, not their gender difference. Avoid sex stereotyping or arbitrarily assigning a primary or secondary role based on sex.

Though many women will continue to choose traditional occupations such as homemaker or secretary, women should not be type-cast in these roles but shown in a wide variety of professions and trades. Similarly, men should not be shown as constantly subject to the "masculine mystique" in their interests, attitudes, or careers. They should not be made to feel that their self-worth depends entirely upon their income level or the status level of their jobs. They should not be conditioned to believe that a man ought to earn more than a woman or that he ought to be the sole support of a family.

An attempt should be made to break job stereotypes for both women and men. No job should be considered sex-typed. Women with a profession should be shown at all administrative levels, including the top levels. Women should be portrayed in positions of authority over men and over other women, and there should be no assumption that a man loses face or that a woman encounters difficulty if the employer or supervisor is a woman. All work should be treated as honorable and worthy of respect; no job or job choices should be downgraded. Instead, women and men should be offered more options than were available to them when work was stereotyped by sex.

Both men and women should be shown engaged in home maintenance activities, ranging from cooking and housecleaning to washing a car and making household repairs. Sometimes the man should be shown preparing the meals, doing the laundry, or diapering the baby, while the woman builds bookcases or takes out the trash.

Girls should be shown as possessing, and exercising, the same options as boys in their play and career choices. In school materials, girls should be encouraged to show an interest in mathematics, mechanical skills, and active sports, for example, while boys should never be made to feel ashamed of an interest in poetry, art, or music—or an aptitude for cooking, sewing, or child care.

Members of both sexes should be represented as whole human beings with human strengths and weaknesses, not "masculine" or "feminine" ones. However, to simply remove stereotypic information from books serves only to lessen stereotypes and not to increase understanding of the systemic nature of oppression. For without an understanding of the historic patriarchal roots of sexist oppression, an understanding of the present is impossible, nor is a truly feminist vision of a humane future society possible. Textbooks should present information about both historic and current discrimination against women at whatever level the students can understand.

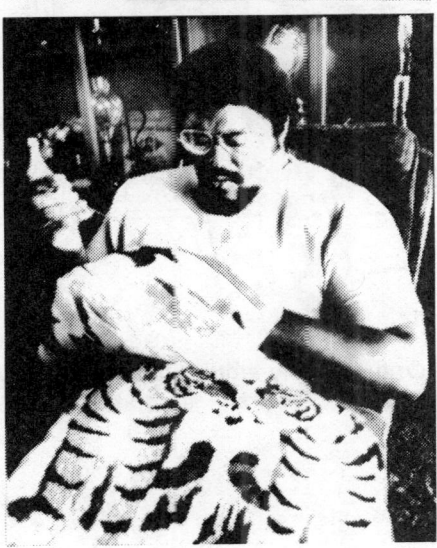

Non traditional work or hobbies can be shown to help dispel sex role stereotypes.

A SEXIST TEXTBOOK IS: one that suggests to children that their lifetime options, capabilities, and behaviors are defined or limited by their sex. Textbooks do this quantitatively—by underrepresenting females—and they do it qualitatively—in the following ways.

**FOUR TEXTBOOK AREAS TO EXAMINE FOR SEXISM—
AND MANY QUESTIONS TO PONDER**

I CHARACTERIZATION

One of many stereotypes in a *Distar Reading Program* textbook.

I CHARACTERIZATION

1. Does the textbook **stereotype human traits and activities** along sex lines? (While some females may display so-called "feminine" traits and perform "feminine" activities, so should some males. When taken as a whole, textbook characters should dispel stereotypic assumptions by having females and males share traits and activities from both the columns below.)

Male Stereotypes	Female Stereotypes
Active	Passive
Brave	Frightened
Strong	Weak
Rough	Gentle
Competitive	Giving up easily
Inventive	Unoriginal
Intelligent, Logical	Silly, Illogical
Quiet, Easygoing	Shrewish, Nagging
Decisive, Problem-solving	Confused
Messy	Neat
Tall	Short
Mechanical	Inept
Independent	Dependent
Leader, Innovator	Follower, Conformer
Expressing anger	Controlling anger
Unemotional	Emotional
Playing or working outdoors	Playing or working indoors
Unconcerned about appearance	Concerned about appearance
As parent, playing with children	As parent, nurturing children
Having innate need for adventure	Having innate need for marriage and motherhood

2. Does the textbook display the following **sex stereotyped occupations?** For females—Housewife, Nurse, Teacher, Secretary, Librarian, Sewer of clothing, Maid, Airline steward, Volunteer. There are no stereotyped occupations for males, except that males in most of the so-called "female occupations" are not considered properly "masculine."

(Both sexes should be presented in non-traditional, as well as in traditional, occupations. Both should be shown in leadership, as well as in supportive, positions. Even though this will show society the way it might be, rather than the way it is, such images are necessary to create suitable role models for young people. However, the truth about existing job discrimination based upon sex must also be included in the textbook.)

3. Does the textbook have **stereotypic storylines** which characterize people

based on their sex? For example:

    A. Are problems confronted and solved as often by females as by males? (This is rare in older copyright books.)

    B. Do "rites of passage" stories about a boy becoming a man through participation in an ordeal or physical trial make children equate "manhood" with brute strength? (Such all-too-common tales damage the self-image of many boys and promote a macho, militaristic mentality particularly dangerous in a nuclear age.)

    C. Are sex integrated activities and friendships among children and adults portrayed? (If not, the textbook is subtly deprecating the goal of people accepting each other because of their human qualities, not because of their gender.)

    D. Does the textbook portray only nuclear family units? (If so, many children will feel that their own families and lifestyles are not quite legitimate. Texts should portray single parent households, divorced families, extended families, etc.)

    E. Must girls prove themselves by some extraordinary feat in order to be accepted by boys? (e.g., Do they have to hit the winning run, or in some other way fit into male standards of success? We need books which develop more meaningful definitions of success.)

    F. Does the story line imply that being a "tomboy" is acceptable as long as the character eventually becomes a "proper young lady"? (Many new stories feature enterprising, active girls but show only traditional older women. This gives mixed messages to young people.)

    G. Do the stories in the text exclude explanations of historic and current sexism in society? (Textbooks should develop children's concern for the ongoing struggle for full social equity for all. Omission of such information can reinforce existing stereotypes.)

4. Does the author's **perspective** result in stereotypic characterizations?

(If the author's perception is that males and females are endowed with different traits through nature—rather than through nurture, or socialization—then the textbook will severely limit descriptions of people to prescribed sex roles.)

The caption in this 1975 Social Science textbook says: "People know how to make and use tools."

II LANGUAGE AND TERMINOLOGY

Does the textbook use the English language in ways that demean or subsume females? This can occur in the following ways:

1. Are male nouns, pronouns, or suffixes used to represent both sexes? Does the text avoid the use of "masculine" or "feminine" titles or descriptions when such words are not referring to a specific sex, or if the sex is unknown?

Instead of	**The Text Might Say**
Men and Nations	People and Nations
Forefathers	Founders or Ancestors
Cro-Magnon man	Cro-Magnon people
Each student must read his book.	All students must read their books.
A good nurse respects her patients.	Good nurses respect their patients.
When a child reads he can . . .	When children read they can . . .
	or When a child reads he or she can . . .

Book titles like the one on the above 1974 textbook are now being replaced by titles like *People in America*.

Instead of	The Text Might Say
Middleman	Go-between or Trader
Man-sized	Large or Huge
Manmade	Synthetic or Manufactured
Brotherhood	Community or Friendship
Cameraman	Camera operator or Photographer
Manpower	People power or Personnel
Freshman	First-year student
Mailman	Letter carrier
Businessman	Business person
Saleswoman	Salesperson
Fireman	Firefighter
Foreman	Supervisor
Repairman	Repairer or Repair person

2. Does the text use equivalent constructions when presenting both sexes in similar roles?

Instead of	The Text Might Say
Man and wife	Man and woman or Husband and wife
Men and ladies	Men and women or Gentlemen and ladies
John Smith and his wife	John and Mary Smith
The men and their wives	The husbands and wives or The married couples
Coaches Brant and Patty Jones were working out their teams.	Coaches Brant and Jones were working out their teams. or Coaches Ben Brant and Patty Jones . . .

3. Does the text use women's first names in places where full names for males would ordinarily be used?

Instead of	The Text Might Say
Frederick Douglass and Harriet Tubman were great Americans. Douglass was a writer, orator, and leader while Harriet bravely . . .	Frederick Douglass and Harriet Tubman were great Americans. Douglass was a writer, orator, and leader while Tubman bravely . . .

4. Does the text use words or expressions which ascribe particular human traits only to males or only to females, as do the terms below?

Feminine	The fair sex
Masculine	Sissy
Hussy	Tomboy
Dowager	Good, Mary! You think like a man!
Spinsterish	Don't cry, Joey. Take it like a man!
Womanish	Sit up and act like a lady!

5. Does the text use descriptors or diminutive word endings to denote a female? (The descriptors "lady" or "woman" for example, should not be used before a profession to denote the sex of the professional.)

Instead of	The Text Might Say
Sculptress	Sculptor
Poetess	Poet
Actress	Actor
Waitress	Waiter
Aviatrix	Aviator
Heroine	Hero
Lady coach	Coach
Woman lawyer	Lawyer

It is difficult to stereotype women who actively fight for their rights. But too often such women are simply ignored in textbooks.

6. Does the text describe females in terms of their appearance or their relationship to men in ways that would not ordinarily be used in describing males?

Instead of	The Text Might Say
Principal Warren Sweet and his attractive, blonde wife Mary . . .	Principal Warren Sweet and Mary Sweet. . . . or Grey-haired, handsome Principal Warren Sweet and blonde, attractive wife, Mary Sweet . . .
School Board members voting "no" were Sue Sennis, wife of Dr. John Sennis, and Lew Morgan.	School Board members voting "no" were Sue Sennis and Lew Morgan. or School Board members voting "no" were Sue Sennis, wife of Dr. John Sennis, and Lew Morgan, husband of mathematician Mary Morgan.

7. Does the text use language implying that men always have control over women, or that women are less important than men?

Instead of	The Text Might Say
Congress finally granted women the vote in 1919.	Women finally won the vote in 1919.
In many ancient Indian societies men allowed women to control the family and the home.	In many ancient Indian societies women controlled the family and the home.
The pioneers faced many hardships while bringing their families along the trail.	Pioneer families faced many hardships while traveling along the trail.

III HISTORICAL BACKGROUND

Does the textbook leave women out of history? This can happen in several ways:

1. Are the achievements of women presented?

2. Are the reasons presented to explain why fewer women than men were achievers in many fields, or were unrecognized despite their achievements?

3. Are the experiences of women during different historical periods presented, or are they ignored as unimportant? (Since history has traditionally been written, studied and taught through a male perspective of what is important, the lives and the concerns of women are usually omitted—or minimized.)

4. When the lives and concerns of women are presented (diaries, letters, and numerous original sources are available to textbook publishers), are women of all races and classes represented?

5. Does the text include the differences, as well as the similarities, in the concerns of women and men, rich women and poor women, white women and women of color?

IV ILLUSTRATIONS—

Do the textbook illustrations demean women in any way? For example:

1. Does the textbook present numerically equal images of males and females? Are they also equal in terms of central placement and activities?

2. Are males always taller than females? Or do both sexes display a variety of heights, shapes, and features?

3. Are similar art styles and colors used for both sexes?

4. Are characters dressed suitably for the activity they are engaged in? (Women rarely do housekeeping in high heels and aprons. Girls usually wear pants in playgrounds, etc.)

5. Do both sexes portray a range of emotions?

6. Are toys of children sex stereotyped?

7. When historic photos and drawings are used that reflect the sexism of their period, do the editorial captions point up the sexism?

Illustrations of females in such roles appear in new textbooks.

Racism In Basal Readers And Other Textbooks, Too

RACISM IS: any attitude, action, or institutional practice which subordinates people because of their color. (Whether racism is intentional or unintentional is beside the point. Only the results are important in judging whether an action, an institution, or a society, is racist.

RACISM IS EVIDENCED IN U.S. SOCIETY BY: statistics which show that racial minorities, when compared to whites, suffer from inferior housing, health, and education, from lower income, and from shorter life spans. The median family income of third world people in the United States is 59 per cent that of white families' median income—and the income gap is *not* closing. Unemployment is double that of whites. Minority adults are 18 to 20 per cent of the population (minority children are about 20 to 22 per cent of the school population), yet minorities hold only 1 per cent of U.S. elective offices and less than 2 per cent of top executive positions in business.

EDUCATION HELPS MAINTAIN RACISM BY: maintaining practices and materials which reinforce and perpetuate a racist society. Textbooks are a key factor. Within societies characterized by racial oppression, books tend to project the views, perspectives, and historical interpretations of the dominating racial group. The books thus reflect the prevailing views of superiority and inferiority. They contain, as well, the justifications developed by the dominating race to rationalize its position of privilege.

Racism in textbooks is not just a problem of blatant portrayals of one race as inferior, and the other as superior. It is also a distorted interpretation of the historical roots and the present condition of discrimination. Therefore, to simply remove stereotypic information from texts serves only to lessen stereotypes, but not to increase understanding of the systemic nature of oppression. Without an accurate understanding of the historical roots of racial oppression and exploitation, an understanding of the present is impossible.

While racism in books distorts reality for children of *both* the dominant and oppressed groups, the effects are different. For the most part, white children lack contact with other racial groups—so the portrayal, in textbooks, of other races as inferior encourages them to develop a self-concept characterized by a feeling of superiority. For children of the dominated group, the textbook portrayals of their group lead toward the development of a negative self-image. To the extent that education fails to expose the mechanisms which maintain the system of privilege for one race and oppression for other races, it serves to perpetuate those inequities.

TEXTBOOKS UNDERREPRESENT MINORITIES: Blacks are about 12 per cent of the total population of the United States; they are a still larger percentage of the youth population. In the 20 largest cities, Blacks average 36 per cent of all public school students. Studies indicate,

Dr. Patricia Bidol has conducted many workshops for educators who wish to become aware of how racism affects education.

however, that in widely used textbooks, Blacks constitute from 7 to 16 per cent of the characters portrayed. Despite significant improvement during the last two decades, Blacks are still very much underrepresented in comparison to their proportion in the population using the books.

In 1976, Dorothy Rainey analyzed 124 stories from 12 textbooks, and found that 69 per cent of all central characters were white and 16 per cent Black (11 per cent were other minority). Black males appeared three times as often as Black females. This confirms other studies showing that the underrepresentation of Black females accounts for the underrepresentation of Blacks in most recent texts.

Latinos represent about 6 per cent of the total population of the United States, but are younger on an average than the white population. Because of the rapid growth of the Latino population, it is expected that they will soon be about 10 per cent of the school students. In 1974, Gwyneth Britton documented the underrepresentation of each of the major Latino groups. Hispanic Americans collectively represented, as major characters, 1 per cent of the stories in reading texts, far less than their presence in the U.S. population.

Asian and Pacific Island Americans are about 0.7 per cent of the population. Unlike Blacks and Latinos, however, their group is *not* underrepresented. Gwyneth Britton found they are central characters in about 1.3 per cent of the total number of stories.

Native Americans represent about 0.4 per cent of the total population and are *over*represented in reading textbooks. For example, in her 1974 analysis discussed above, Gwyneth Britton found that Native Peoples were central characters in about 2 per cent of the total, but were far more frequently male than female. She found that males appeared as major characters more than three and a half times as often as females. Georgia Napier's study found that 63 per cent of Indian characters were male.

But the problem is not *quantity*. The *quality* of the stories is generally the problem. For example, Napier found that Native American characters are seldom portrayed in contemporary circumstances. Only one out of the 20 textbooks she analyzed portrayed the life of an American Indian *after* the Second World War.

Robert Moore and Arlene Hirschfelder, in their 1977 study of "Indian" imagery in children's books, also found that the image of Native Americans was limited to the past, "suggesting to children that Indians do not exist in the present or that, if they do, they are less 'Indian' today."

A RACIST TEXTBOOK IS: one that makes minority children feel that they, their language, viewpoints, and culture are inferior, and makes white children feel that they are superior. Textbooks can do this quantitatively—through underrepresentation—or qualitatively, in the following ways.

FIVE TEXTBOOK AREAS TO EXAMINE FOR RACISM— AND MANY QUESTIONS TO PONDER

White, male feelings of superiority can be reinforced by textbooks which underrepresent women and people of color.

I CHARACTERIZATION

Does the textbook stereotype third world characters? (Bear in mind that stereotypes are often contradictory, e.g., the "Wicked Dragon Lady" is one stereotyped image and the "Sweet China Doll" is another contradictory stereotype. However, both make the female character less than fully human—which is exactly the purpose of any stereotype. Stereotypes have always been used to justify oppression. The "heathen, savage Indian" stereotype was useful to "Christian, civilized settlers" who wanted to decimate Indian people to more readily take away their land. While new stereotypes are developed to meet changing times, old ones rarely die—they just acquire more sophisticated nuances.)

Stereotypic characterizations occur because of:

1. **Language usage** (e.g., "the Happy-Go-Lucky Black," "the Inscrutable Chinese," "the Lazy Mexican," "the Knife-toting Puerto Rican").

2. **Implying sameness.** The implication that all members of a minority group live in set places, work in like occupations, and/or have similar socioeconomic status (e.g., Reservation Indians, Migrant Farmworkers Chicanos, Chinese Laundrymen, Ghetto Blacks).

3. **Omission of minority perspectives** (e.g., the oppression is described, but the struggle of third world people against the oppression is omitted, or the implication is given that a minority group is accepting of inferior status).

4. **A story line** in which:

   A. The goal of the third world character is to be accepted by whites.

   B. Whites accept a third world character after s/he performs superhuman feats or exhibits super-human forgiveness.

   C. The implication is given that minority persons—rather than white society—are responsible for their own poverty and that if only they learned to "speak good English" or to get a "good education," all will be well. (This blaming-the-victim approach to poverty occurs in social study texts as well as in basal readers.)

   D. A benevolent white person solves the problem for the third world character, and all is well thereafter. (White racism and societal discrimination are never mentioned, and the implication is given that third world people are less capable than whites.)

Illustrations like the above lead children to believe that all Indians wear feathers and are fierce.

II LANGUAGE AND TERMINOLOGY

(credit note: The following is excerpted from Racism in the English Language *by Robert B. Moore. For availability of the entire booklet, see p. 104.)*

An integral part of any culture is its language. Language not only develops in conjunction with a society's historical, economic, and political evolution, but also reflects that society's attitudes and thinking. Language not only *expresses* ideas and concepts but actually *shapes* thought. If one accepts that our dominant white culture is racist, then one would expect our language—an indispensable transmitter of culture—to be racist as well. Whites, as the dominant group, are not subjected to the same abusive characterization by our language as are people of color.

1. **Obvious Bigotry:** Are terms used such as *nigger, spook, chink, spick?* (While these may be facing increased social disdain, they certainly are very much alive.) If the terms appear in literature (e.g., "nigger Jim" in *Huckleberry Finn)* does editorial matter make clear to young readers that such language is racist and unacceptable?

2. **Color Symbolism:** The symbolism of *white* as positive and *black* as negative is pervasive in our culture, and the black/white words used below are an example.

> Some may blackly (angrily) accuse him of trying to blacken (defame) the English language, to give it a black eye (a mark of shame) by writing such black words (hostile). They may denigrate (to cast aspersions; to darken) him by accusing him of being blackhearted (malevolent), of having a black outlook (pessimistic, dismal) on life, of being a blackguard (scoundrel)—which would certainly be a black mark (detrimental fact) against him. The preceding is of course a white lie (not intended to cause harm).

> "Good guys" wear white hats and ride white horses, "bad guys" wear black hats and ride black horses. Angels are white, and devils are black. A dictionary definition of *black* includes "without any moral light or goodness, evil, wicked, indicating disgrace, sinful," while that of *white* includes "morally pure, spotless, innocent, free from evil intent."

> Three of the dictionary definitions of *white* are "fairness of complexion, purity, innocence." These definitions affect the standards of beauty in our culture, in which whiteness represents the ideal or the norm. "Blondes have more fun" and "Wouldn't you really rather be a blonde?" are sexist in their attitudes toward women generally, but they are racist white standards when applied to third world women.

3. **Politics and Terminology:** *Culturally deprived, economically disadvantaged,* and *underdeveloped* are other terms which mislead and distort our awareness of reality. The application of the term *culturally deprived* to third world children in this society reflects a value judgment. It assumes that the dominant whites are cultured and all others are without culture. Such terms place the responsibility for their own condition on those being so described. This is known as "Blaming the Victim." It places responsibility for poverty on the victims of poverty. It removes the blame from those in power who benefit from—and continue to permit—poverty.

Still another problem involves the use of the misleading terms *non-white, minority,* or *third world*. (These terms are discussed under "Terminology" on p. 41.)

4. **"Loaded" Words:** Many words lead to a demeaning characterization of groups of people. For instance, Columbus, it is said, "discovered" America. The word *discover* is defined as "to gain sight or knowledge of something previously unseen or unknown." Thus, a continent inhabited by millions of human beings cannot be "discovered."

Eurocentric "loaded words" are also apparent in the usage of *victory* and *massacre* to describe the battles between Native Americans and whites. Native American victories are invariably defined as *massacres,* while the indiscriminate killing, extermination, and plunder of Native American nations by EuroAmericans is defined as *victory.*

Conflict among diverse peoples within African nations are often referred to as

The book caption reads: "Balboa climbed a mountain . . . and discovered the Pacific Ocean . . ." Since "discover" means "to see something previously unknown," this caption ignores the knowledge of millions of Indian people who knew all about the Pacific.

tribal warfare, while conflicts among the diverse peoples within European countries are never described in such terms. If the rivalries between the Ibo and the Hausa and Yoruba in Nigeria are described as *tribal*, why not the rivalries between Serbs and Slavs in Yugoslavia, or Basques and Southern Spaniards in Spain? Perfectly good words such as *jungle* and *hut* can acquire racist connotations when they are constantly associated with "uncivilized" peoples. The word *jungle*, for example, may be used to excuse European domination as "civilizing the wild or primitive" African. UNESCO urges that the term *jungle* be replaced with the phrase *wooded savanna*. The word *hut*, when used in dictionaries or other books to indicate that third world dwellings are crude or temporary, forces associations that are racist, not to mention invalid. It would be preferable to use *home* or *dwelling*, preceded by *temporary* should that be the case. The word *native* must likewise be used and defined with care so that it is not confined to people of color.

5. Qualifiers: Words that would normally have positive connotations can have entirely different meanings when used in a racial context. For example, a 1968 *New York Times* article reporting on an address by Lyndon Johnson stated, "The President spoke to the well-dressed Negro officials and their wives." In what similar circumstances can one imagine a reporter finding it necessary to note that an audience of white government officials was "well-dressed"? Other qualifiers frequently used to describe minorities when they would not be similarly used to describe whites are: *intelligent, articulate, qualified*.

6. Names: Third world characters frequently are given "funny" names (e.g., "Chief Five Cents"), or they are frequently known by their first names, while whites are known by two names. Many books merely leave characters of color nameless.

7. We-They-People: The statement, "We want our Black citizens to share all the benefits of U.S. society," implies *we* are all *non-Blacks*. "New Yorkers are handling their Puerto Rican community nicely," implies Puerto Ricans are not New Yorkers. "The people watched the slaves work," implies slaves are not *people*. "The southern students did not want to be thought of as 'rednecks,'" should read, "The southern white students. . . ." White writers constantly make statements like those above, unconsciously implying that "we-us" whites are the real Americans and that "they" don't count.

Page 33 says: "The Middle Belt . . . is part Moslem, part Christian and part pagan." Can a U.S. child respect African religions if they are labelled "pagan"?

III HISTORICAL ACCURACY

While a number of respected white and minority scholars are knowledgeable about third world history, the average educator has received little training in this area. Traditionally, third world history, like women's history, has been excluded from most curriculums. Therefore, checking up on historical authenticity requires the input of knowledgeable scholars or a careful reading of those books which offer perspectives and information missing from history texts. (A useful instrument and a bibliography to aid such a search can be found in *Stereotypes, Distortions and Omissions in U.S. History Textbooks*, published by the Council. See p. 104.)

1. Are there significant **omissions** in the textbook?

    A. Are the contributions of minority groups to the life and culture of the United States fully included?

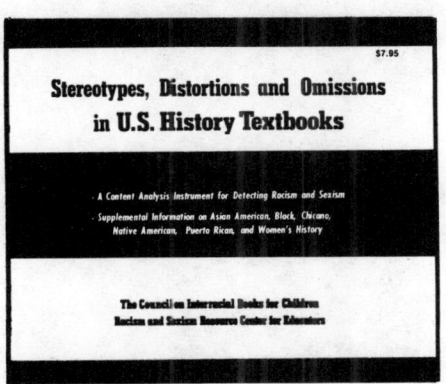

Does the text make readers understand how much bitter struggle was needed to eliminate signs like this?

B. Are the achievements of a particular minority group in the development of its *own* society included? (The point is, Indians should not only be congratulated for giving "us" corn and tomatoes, but for the things they accomplished of significance to their own peoples.)

C. Are the special problems and the varied lives of minority group women included? Are the similarities and diversities of their lives and the lives of white women discussed?

D. Is the history of this land and the people who lived on it prior to the "discovery" of Columbus included?

E. Is the long history of racism included? (The racism of U.S. laws, courts, business practices, police, lynch mobs, segregationists, etc., is often ignored or glossed over by textbooks.) Are the reasons for the development and the perpetuation of ghettos explored?

2. Are there significant **distortions** in the textbook?

A. Does the text accurately describe the various strategies by which people of color have resisted, and continue to resist, discrimination, economic exploitation, and other forms of oppression?

B. Is the colonial experience glorified as being beneficial to the third world group or country, rather than beneficial to the colonizing country or business interests of the colonizer? (Stories or history textbooks often suggest that Africans, Puerto Ricans, Filipinos, etc., are better off than they were before European takeover of their countries. Or they suggest that the third world people could not properly govern themselves or educate their children until whites came and taught them these skills.)

3. Is there a **Eurocentric perspective** in the textbook?

A. Is the history recounted from the viewpoint of what was advantageous to whites or how events appeared to whites?

B. Are the minority heros and leaders in the textbook the people who acted on behalf of their own people? Or are they described in terms of the help they gave to white interests?

IV CULTURAL AUTHENTICITY

Mary Gloyne Byler

It is extremely difficult to grow up in any one culture and to be able to authentically depict another culture. As Native American critic, Mary Gloyne Byler (Cherokee), states in *American Indian Authors for Young Readers:*

> While non-Indian authors may produce well-written and entertaining children's books featuring American Indians, there is little in their stories that tells us much about American Indians. We do learn what non-Indians imagine Indians to be, or think they should be.
>
> There is more to being an American Indian—Apache, Seneca, Hopi, or whatever tribe—than can be acquired through an act of will, a course of study, or discovering an Indian ancestor somewhere in the family tree. It is not an intellectual choice. In short, being Indian is growing up Indian: it is a way of life, a way of thinking and being. Shaped by their own life experiences, non-Indians lack the feelings and insights essential to a valid representation of what it means to be an American Indian.

Charles Gordone, the Black playwright, had one of his stage characters put it even more succinctly: "There's more to being Black than meets the eye."

For the above reasons, multicultural reviewing teams are strongly recommended for analyzing textbooks in terms of cultural authenticity.

1. Is a **white perspective** used to evaluate the culture and customs of the minority group?

    A. Is civilization equated with technology?

    B. Are third world cultures evaluated on the basis of their material objects, such as pottery, homes, jewelry?

    C. Are the highly complex religions of third world peoples treated respectfully?

    D. Are the different value systems, such as the Native American belief in communal land ownership and use, presented without the implication that the white value system is superior?

2. Are minority cultures and customs **distorted** or **trivialized**?

    A. Are a few customs, which appear strange or exotic to EuroAmericans, emphasized as though there were no greater depth and meaning to the culture as a whole? (An example are texts which tell of Chinese New Year festivals, with dragons, or of the Mexican piñata parties, while ignoring the basic factors of Asian American or Chicano culture.)

    B. Are folk tales distorted because whites apply the story to EuroAmerican concepts and thus lose or change the meaning of the tale? (Many "Br'er Rabbit" stories were really about slaves tricking their "masters." And many Native American folktales were meant to teach young people some particular idea or value.)

3. Are significant facts about third world cultures **omitted**?

    A. Are the family systems—which usually stress loyalty, solidarity, and respect within the family above individual interests—presented?

    B. Is the essential reverence for life of third world cultures, as expressed through their music, dancing, religion, art, and literature presented? (It is important that texts counteract the racist assumption that human life is "cheap" to third world peoples.)

    C. Are the alternatives to present U.S. lifestyles and values posed by the alternative lifestyles and values of third world groups presented as potentially valuable (e.g., the Native American concepts of sharing community resources and of respecting the earth)?

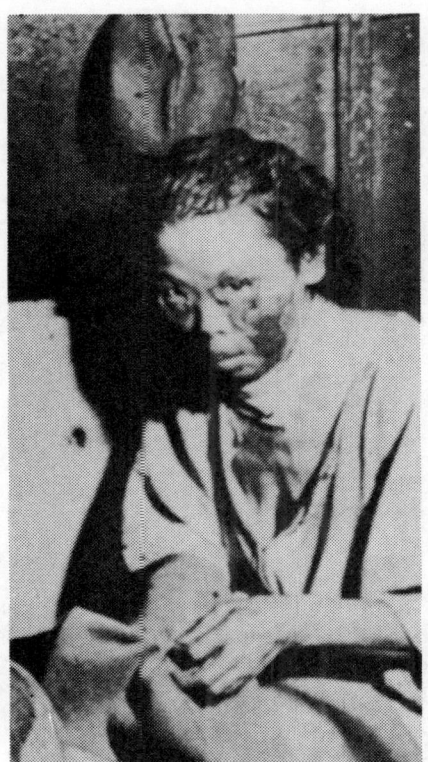

For Americans who dropped the H-bomb on two large Japanese cities to accuse people of color of holding human life "cheap" is beyond comment.

V ILLUSTRATIONS

1. Do minorities comprise 20 to 25 per cent of illustrated central characters and of background characters? Do females comprise 50 per cent of the minority characters depicted?

2. Are minorities shown in leadership positions and, at times, directing or leading white people?

3. Are facial characteristics accurately and sensitively drawn to show variety of skin tones, hair textures and styles, eye shapes, etc.?

4. Do illustrations reinforce or dispel racial stereotypes?

5. Are the socioeconomic settings and lifestyles of third world cultures illustrated in as varied ways as they are for whites?

6. Is the clothing depicted suitable for the occasion? Or is it merely a prop to establish racial identity?

AFROAMERICANS

(credit note: The following points are based upon: Racism in the English Language *by Robert B. Moore, published by the Council;* Starting Out Right: Choosing Books About Black People for Young Children, *edited by Bettye I. Latimer; and many articles and book reviews written by AfroAmericans and published by the Council in its magazine, the* Bulletin. *See p. 104 for availability of these materials.)*

I CHARACTERIZATION

1. Does the text contain any of the stereotypes listed below?

Male Stereotypes
the shuffling, eye-rolling, fearful, superstitious comic
the gentle, self-sacrificing older man
the athletic super-jock
the smooth-talking con man
the super-stud
the stupid, but comical, little boy
the rough, dangerous criminal
the loudly-dressed, happy-go-lucky buffoon
the exotic primitive

Female Stereotypes
the big-bosomed "mammy," loyal to whites
the big, bossy mother or maid—commander of the household
the sexy temptress
the stupid, but sweet, little girl
the tragic mulatto

This old stereotype is alive and well on TV, in movies, on greeting cards and in at least one 1980 children's book we've seen.

Occupational Stereotypes: chauffeur; cook; maid; laundry worker; elevator operator; waiter (these occupational stereotypes are based on historic racism, which relegated Blacks to menial positions, and on current racism, which continues to keep a disproportionate number of Blacks in the same low-paying jobs); the unemployed ghetto dweller; preacher; undertaker; athlete; entertainer.

The stereotypes listed above are blatant and are no longer common in educational materials, but reflections are still found in comic books, in movies, and in adult literature, so that children are aware of them. Therefore, considerable care must be taken lest *any* stereotype is reinforced.

2. Does the **story line** characterize Blacks in negative ways?

   A. Are the problems in the story handled by the Black protagonist? Other AfroAmericans? Or by benevolent whites? (The last is a common racist theme.)

   B. Is the Black protagonist sacrificed for the sake of a white person? Is the Black protagonist more concerned about a white child than about other Black characters? (This may be satisfying to white egos but is nevertheless a racist theme.)

C. Does the story imply that getting an education and/or ridding oneself of so-called Black dialect will pave the way for "success" in life? (Well educated Blacks experience racial oppression, and they earn considerably less than similarly educated whites.)

D. Does the Black protagonist have to perform extraordinary feats (e.g., super-athletic, super-brave, super-smart, super-patient-and-forgiving) in order to win acceptance by whites?

E. Are AfroAmericans who speak "Black English" presented as less intelligent than characters who speak standard English (whatever that is)?

F. Are there a variety of positive Black role models for both sexes?

G. Do Black characters show preference for white culture and white characters?

H. Are ghettos the only environment in which Blacks are depicted?

3. Do **omissions** distort the characterizations?

A. If AfroAmericans are depicted living in poverty, is the situation described as being their own fault? Or are social causes—such as racism and discrimination—examined?

B. If injustice is presented, do AfroAmerican characters passively accept it? Or do they, in some fashion, struggle or resist? (Black passivity is historically false, and it is false today.)

C. Are the strengths and supportive characteristics of Black families of all kinds—extended families, nuclear families, single parent families—shown? Or is there a concentration on broken homes and social pathology?

D. If the story presents an incident of racial prejudice, is it described as an isolated act of a bigot? Or as typical of what constantly occurs to Black people in U.S. society? Or does the author omit any comment?

4. Does a white **perspective** distort the characterization of the Blacks?

A. Given the historical period in which an event takes place, are the AfroAmerican perspectives somehow included? (Authors have innumerable devices for doing this subtly, without destroying credibility or artistic integrity.)

B. When there is interplay between white and AfroAmerican characters, is the viewpoint of the minority characters as clear to readers as is the viewpoint and values of whites?

Black resistance to injustice was typified by the Montgomery bus boycott, sparked by Rosa Parks and joined by Dr. Martin Luther King, Jr. It is important that more stories be told about people who fight for their rights.

II LANGUAGE AND TERMINOLOGY

1. If dialect or slang is used, does it serve a purpose? Will its rhythm, cadence, and words ring true to Black people?

2. If the story uses "Black English" is it presented in a way that will cause young white readers to feel disrespectful, or young AfroAmerican readers to feel inferior?

While this is from a popular amusement park, not a textbook, textbooks issued in the late 1970's still played up the same image in their cover illustrations.

3. Is the word *black* used pejoratively? (In *Roget's Thesaurus,* "black" has 60 negative—and not a single positive—connotations. Thus, bias against Black people is reinforced by the negative meaning of *blackness,* and children are influenced to make undesirable associations. The word *white* has 44 positive synonyms and 10 very mildly negative synonyms, e.g., whitewash.) Or does the author find positive ways to describe black skin and hair, and beauty?

4. Except when necessary for historical accuracy, are obviously racist words, or terms now rejected by Black people, used (e.g., nigger, colored, Negro)? If they are used for historical accuracy, is an editorial explanation offered?

5. Are whites called *people* while Blacks are called *slaves* or are omitted from the meaning of the sentence? (e.g., "The people drank their juleps while the slaves worked." or "Southerners thought slavery and Christianity were compatible." In the latter sentence the word *white* should be inserted before "Southerners.")

6. Are value laden terms used, such as *culturally deprived* or *disadvantaged* (why not *culturally different, poor,* or *economically exploited)*?

7. Is the term *non-white* used to describe groups of people? If so, whiteness is being used as the standard or norm against which to measure others.

8. Do Blacks "grin" and show "gleaming white teeth" while whites merely "smile," or "laugh"? Is black hair described in derogatory fashion (e.g., kinky, nappy)?

9. Do "loaded words" describe Africa or Africans (e.g., *darkest, jungle, hut, primitive, cannibal, pagan, tribe)*? Are European-imposed names, such as "Hottentots" and "Bushmen" used? These are offensive to Africans and are incorrect. In their place, use "Khai-Khoin" and "San." "Kaffir" is a Muslim term meaning *infidel,* and is also offensive.

If the term *tribe* is used exclusively in relation to Africans, and never to European people, it connotes bias. *Tribe* is an imprecise concept, and experts do not agree on its correct meaning, or to what scale unit the word is applicable. A. Babs Fafunwa, of Nigeria, at a UNESCO meeting, remarked feelingly: "How an ethnic group with two or ten million people in East or West Africa, with a parliamentary government, can be described as a *tribe* and not the Irish, the Scots, the Welsh, the French, or the English, still baffles the non-European."

10. Are qualifying adjectives used that would be superfluous if used to describe whites in similar situations? (See p. 43.)

11. Is the term *boy* used to describe adult males and *girl* to describe adult females (e.g., "My cleaning girl comes every Friday.")? Such blatantly offensive terminology is not in new materials but still appears in books on library shelves and in old films shown repeatedly on TV. While such language is also sexist, it has been used in racist fashion for hundreds of years. If it appears in literature, editorial comment should be offered and class discussion initiated.

12. Are divisive words used (e.g., *mulatto, quadroon)*? Black people of all shades and heritage proudly call themselves *Black, AfroAmerican,* or *African American.*

13. If full names are given for whites, is that also done for Black characters? Are the names of Blacks totally omitted?

III HISTORICAL ACCURACY

1. Is the Black perspective on historical events included?

2. Are African roots of culture and history included where applicable? Are African civilizations prior to contact with Europe included?

3. Are the achievements and contributions of AfroAmericans in developing the wealth and culture of U.S. society presented?

4. Is the resistance of Black people to slavery and later forms of discrimination omitted or distorted?

5. Are AfroAmerican heros who fought for their people included, whether or not the heros are "acceptable" to white society?

6. Is Civil Rights legislation stressed while lack of enforcement is ignored? Similarly, are gains of Blacks emphasized while their meager economic advances and absence of national decision making power are omitted?

IV CULTURAL AUTHENTICITY

1. If stories are set in an African or Caribbean nation, are the values and belief systems which make up its particular culture accurately described? (Obviously, this evaluation must be made by people thoroughly familiar with the particular culture or nation.)

An entire page is devoted to "Livingstone (above) and Stanley" in the 1978 *The Afro-Asian World*, yet no mention is made of the destruction that Stanley wreaked on African villages.

2. If stories are set in the United States, is there a recognition that there exists a variety of AfroAmerican lifestyles, cultures, and speech patterns, e.g., those from the West Indies, from the rural South, from Northern urban ghettos, etc.?

3. Does a basal reader include originally "white" stories or poems—revising the illustrations to show Black characters in order to meet a multicultural "quota"—instead of finding culturally authentic stories by AfroAmerican authors? (Some simple stories for very young children *are* acceptable that way, but a culturally authentic story is always preferable.)

V ILLUSTRATIONS

1. Are Black features, skin tones, hair styles and textures, in their full variety, presented accurately without exaggeration? Or are they white features covered with a tint?

2. Are the clothes worn by AfroAmericans suitable to the occasion?

3. In group illustrations, are the Black characters as prominent as whites? Or are they placed in the background?

4. Are Black females shown outdoors, active, and in leadership roles? Are Black female children equal in height to male children?

5. Are Blacks illustrated in leadership positions and sometimes shown directing whites?

One example of the many fine artists who draw Black people sensitively.

ASIAN AMERICANS

(credit note: In 1976 the Council published the results of a study by Asian American book reviewers who evaluated available children's books on Asian American themes. With two exceptions the books were found to be racist, sexist, and elitist. The full study, with book reviews, is available. See p. 104.)

I CHARACTERIZATION

1. Does the text include **stereotypes** such as those below?

From this still popular 1938 "classic," generations of children have come to believe that all Asians are a putrid yellow, have slits for eyes, look alike and act foolishly.

Male Stereotypes

smiling, polite, and small
servile, bowing
bucktoothed and squinty-eyed
mystical, inscrutable, and wise
expert in martial arts
exotic foreigner
sinister, sly
places no value on human life
model minority, who worked hard and "made it"
super-student

Female Stereotypes

sweet, well-behaved girl
sexy, sweet "China Doll"
sexy, evil "Dragon Lady"
overbearing, old-fashioned grandmother

Occupational Stereotypes

Chinese American men are laundrymen, restaurant workers, or curio shop owners; Japanese men are gardeners or florists; Filipino men are "houseboys." Women are not occupationally stereotyped. (In past years historical racism allowed Asian Americans to work only in a limited number of occupations—cooking or laundry work—which white, male workers spurned as being "unmanly." Even today, many Chinese can find work only in the kitchens of Chinese restaurants or in garment sweatshops. Depending upon the setting, time and place, an author might include some of this information to explain why an Asian American character is in a stereotyped occupation. In any case, children must not be led to believe that occupations are linked to race.)

2. Does the **story line** characterize Asian Americans negatively?

   A. Are successful outcomes to problems dependent on a white character, or are they handled by the Asian American protagonist or other Asian Americans?

   B. Does the protagonist have to make an all-or-nothing choice between traditional Asian culture or "modern" U.S. culture? Or is the possibility of choosing elements from each shown? (Books often confuse the root culture with the Asian American culture.)

   C. Are the characters respected on their own terms, or must they "prove" themselves by being extraordinarily outstanding in some way, in order to win approval from whites?

   D. Is the Asian American experience interpreted as a "success" story, giving the false impression that Asian Americans have overcome the oppression against them by dint of hard work and by passively turning the other cheek? Is such behavior represented as a "model" for other third world groups to emulate?

   E. Are positive Asian American role models presented for both sexes?

   F. Is the implication given that learning to speak "good" English and assimilate white ways is all that is needed to become "successful"?

G. If injustice is presented, do the Asian Americans passively accept it? Or do they struggle to overcome it?

H. If the text describes an Asian American child of today, are the realistic experiences and feelings engendered by living in a white racist society included? Or could the same story be about a white child?

3. Does the **perspective** result in negative characterization?

Is the Asian American behavior judged solely from a white perspective? Or is the behavior of the white characters also judged from an Asian or Asian American viewpoint?

II LANGUAGE AND TERMINOLOGY

1. Are the names of the characters authentic or do they parody real Asian names (e.g., Gilbert and Sullivan's "Nanki-Poo")? Are full names of Asian Americans given when full names of whites appear?

2. Are speech patterns parodied? Is there the "Confucius-say," stilted speech syndrome? Do characters speak in hyperbolized eloquence with confused "r's" and "l's" ("rots of ruck," "flied lice," "honorable sir")?

3. Are "loaded words" such as *inscrutable, shy, smiling, bowing, sly, dainty, slinky, squinty-eyed, pigeon-toed* used as descriptives?

4. Are derogatory terms such as *Japs, Chinks, Gooks* used? If so, is their offensive nature made clear to young readers?

5. If the story contains both Asian Americans and EuroAmericans, is the word *people* used to refer solely to the whites?

6. Are Chinese and Japanese Americans referred to as "Chinese" and "Japanese" even when they are second and third generation Americans?

This U.P.I. photo was taken in Phoenix, Arizona in 1935. Internment of Japanese in the 1940's was the result of decades of anti-Asian racism—a fact rarely noted in textbooks.

III HISTORICAL ACCURACY

1. If historical reasons for Asian emigration are presented, do they include the active recruitment of Asians by U.S. business interests and of the particular harsh conditions in the homelands which led to the emigration? Or are young readers led to believe that Asians came to the United States simply to get rich quickly?

2. Does the book ignore the legal and de facto racism practiced against Asians and Asian Americans in a systematic way over many years in the United States?

3. If oppression is described, is Asian American resistance also described?

4. Is the internment of Japanese Americans in concentration camps during World War II not mentioned, or dismissed as an unfortunate aberration of U.S. democratic traditions? Or is it presented as a logical extension of years of racist oppression on the West Coast and also as profitable to many whites who lived there at the time?

IV CULTURAL AUTHENTICITY

1. Are Asian Americans portrayed as "imitation" Americans or as Asian foreigners? Or are they portrayed as people whose experience in the United States has generated a unique and distinctive Asian American culture, which differs from the root Asian culture?

2. Is the full range of a particular culture depicted, or is it trivialized and exoticized by dwelling solely on the Chinese New Year, on the Japanese O-bon festival, or on any one particular part of a complex cultural whole?

3. Are the settings, behavior, speech, and clothing depicted accurately for the historical period and cultural context? (Traditional Chinese or Japanese garments are rarely worn by Asian Americans.)

4. Do the characters presented come from a variety of social and economic levels or, if that is not possible, does the text avoid the implication that all Asian Americans are of the same background?

5. Is the validity of Asian American outlooks, values, and lifestyles respected?

6. Is it implied that Asian peoples place little value on human life?

V ILLUSTRATIONS

1. Are variations in skin tone presented? Or are all Asian Americans colored an unreal yellow?

2. Are differences in facial structure between Asian American individuals and Asian American nationalities depicted? Or are all Asian Americans made to look alike?

3. Are variations in shapes of eyes shown? Or are they all drawn as stereotypically slanted slits—without any pupils?

4. Are hair styles depicted as bowl-style haircuts, pigtails, and other unlikely stereotypes? Or are they varied and contemporary?

5. Are stereotypic props like Fu Manchu mustaches, mandarin jackets, kimonos and obis, buck teeth and horn-rimmed glasses, dragons, kites and paper lanterns, bowed heads and downcast eyes, used to depict Asian Americans?

6. If traditional clothing is shown, is it historically correct, accurately depicted, and appropriate to the occasion?

7. If Asian cities are shown, are they illustrated only in long ago, exotic ways?

8. When "Chinatowns" are shown, are they presented only as tourist spots and exotica? Or are the substandard housing and other ghetto conditions depicted as well?

9. In group illustrations, are Asian Americans centrally placed at times? Are females the same size as males when shown under 14 years of age? Are there roughly equal numbers of females and males?

A page from a nicely illustrated new textbook.

LATINOS OR HISPANIC AMERICANS

(credit note: Mexican Americans, Puerto Ricans, Cuban Americans, and people from other Latin American areas are proportionately the youngest and the fastest growing segment of the U.S. population. The Council conducted two studies of the way this group is portrayed in children's literature. One was a study of 100 books about Puerto Ricans, the other of 200 books about Chicanos. The full studies are available from the Council, see p. 104.)

I CHARACTERIZATION

1. Does the text include **stereotypes** such as those below?

Male Stereotypes

sombrero-wearing, serape-clad, sandaled man or boy
man taking a siesta near a cactus or an overburdened burro
ignorant, cheerful, lazy peon
sneaky, knife-wielding, mustached bandit
humble, big-eyed, poor-but-honest boy
teenage gang member
macho boaster and supreme-commander of household

Female Stereotypes

hard working, poor, submissive, self-sacrificing religious mother of many
sweet, small, shy, gentle girl
sexy, loud, fiery, young woman (who often prefers a white man to Latino men)
undereducated, submissive, nice girl with marriage as a life goal

Occupational Stereotypes

impoverished migrant workers (most Latinos actually live in cities)
unemployed barrio dwellers

2. Does the **story line** result in negative characterizations of the Latinos?

   A. Are problems resolved by the Chicanos, Puerto Ricans, or other Latino characters? Or are problems cleared up by the benevolent intervention of a kind white person?

   B. Does the Latino decide to give up some aspect of his or her root culture in order to achieve happiness or success?

   C. Is it stated or implied that learning "good" English is the individual solution to social problems, such as poverty or inferior education?

   D. Do the characters have to show extraordinary attributes (super-patience, super-honesty, super-athletic skill) in order to win acceptance by whites? Is such "acceptance" posed as a goal in life?

   E. Are the Spanish-speaking characters presented as less than "real Americans"?

   F. Are there positive Latino role models of both sexes? Are the Latinos depicted struggling against oppression?

   G. In poverty situations, is the Latino given full responsibility for surmounting poverty? Or are societal causes explored? Are pat, silly solutions presented? (For example, does a poor, lonely Puerto Rican child who misses his or her "island paradise" adjust to an overcrowded tenement after s/he sees snow for the first time and makes one friend? This standard story line is an insulting way to deal with the reasons for migration and with the problems of poverty in Puerto Rico and the United States.)

    H. If the story is about a contemporary Latino child, do the feelings engendered by living in a racist society appear in the story? Or could the same story be told substituting a white child? (There are some simple stories in which it *is* legitimate to depict *any* child.)

3. Does a white perspective result in negative characterizations?

    A. Are the behavior and culture of the white characters judged from the Latino viewpoint, or is the viewpoint solely that of an Anglo looking down on another culture?

II LANGUAGE AND TERMINOLOGY

1. Is Spanish regarded as equally prestigious and legitimate as English?

2. Are Spanish words, phrases, and names spelled correctly and used appropriately? Are accent marks in proper places?

3. Is "broken English" used as a device to portray a person whose first language is Spanish in a demeaning way?

4. Are "loaded words" used, such as *greasy, lazy, fiery*?

5. If full names of Anglo characters are given, do the Latino characters also have full names?

6. Does a character "lapse" into Spanish when excited? (We've never read of anyone "lapsing" into English.)

III HISTORICAL ACCURACY

Juan "Cheno" Contina, considered a bandit by the U.S., was a hero to his people. He waged guerrilla warfare against "gringos" from 1859 to 1875, trying to regain land taken from Mexico.

JUAN "CHENO" CORTINA 1859
—just before he began to fight back
—poco antes de empezar a resistir

1. Given the historical period in which the story is set, does a description of the events include Chicano, Puerto Rican, or other Latino perspectives?

2. Are the settings, actions, dates, politics, and events described historically accurate? (Section on U.S. History Texts, pp. 86-103, may be useful.)

3. Are there any stories of Mexican accomplishments and civilization prior to the U.S. takeover? Prior to the landing of the Mayflower?

4. Are Chicano contributions to U.S. agronomy and mining included where appropriate?

5. Are Latino struggles against past or present oppression included? Or is oppression ignored or glossed over?

6. Are viewpoints and events critical of U.S. policies or actions omitted from the story when they might logically be included?

7. If the story identifies Mexican, Mexican American, Puerto Rican, or other Latino heros, are they selected because they supported U.S. interests? (Many Latinos who are labelled "zealots" or "bandits" by Anglos are considered heros by their own people.)

8. Are the full reasons for emigration of Latinos to the United States presented? Is an explanation offered for the back and forth travel of Puerto Ricans to the U.S. mainland?

IV CULTURAL AUTHENTICITY

1. Is the root culture (Mexican, Puerto Rican, other) described correctly? Or is it trivialized or distorted by limiting descriptions to fiestas, piñata parties, patron saints, etc.?

2. Is a difference shown between the root culture and the present Chicano or Puerto Rican mainland culture?

3. Is a Spanish name given to someone who in no way (other than by name) seems to be Latino? (Basal readers often use this simplistic device to fill multicultural "quotas." Preferable would be stories presenting authentic Latino cultures.)

4. Are a variety of socioeconomic settings accurately depicted in cultural context?

5. Are cultural factors communicated, such as strong sense of family relationships, sense of honor, respect for elders, responsibility for communal welfare?

V ILLUSTRATIONS

1. Is the racial diversity of Latinos depicted? (Latinos evolve from direct or mixed European, African, and Native "Indian" peoples. Skin tone, therefore, varies from what is called, "white," to what is called, "black." Hair color, hair texture, and facial structure also have numerous variations. Eye color is *not* always brown.)

2. Are "props," such as sombreros, burros, cactus trees avoided?

3. Are barrios shown stereotypically as charming, gay, colorful, postcard-like places?

4. Are costumes or peasant clothes shown in situations where characters would ordinarily wear the same type of contemporary clothing that Anglos would in the same situation?

5. Is the size of females in relation to males shown realistically for their ages? Are females shown outdoors and active?

While many Chicanos are farm workers, the majority are urban dwellers. In both country and city they are generally underpaid. Textbooks should make students understand the relationship between historic racism and low income for Latinos today.

Illustrations like this appear time and again, leading youngsters to believe all Mexicans and Chicanos look this way.

NATIVE AMERICANS

(credit note: Unlike the scarcity of children's stories about Asian Americans, Latinos, and Blacks, there are endless numbers about "Indians." The observations in this section are based upon the following: a booklet by Mary Gloyne Byler (Cherokee), published by the Association on American Indian Affairs; a study called, "Feathers, Tomahawks, and Tipis: A Study of Stereotyped Indian Imagery in Children's Picture Books," by Robert B. Moore and Arlene Hirschfelder, published by the Council; and many books reviewed in Council publications by Native American people. Available Council materials on this topic are listed on p. 104.)

I CHARACTERIZATION

1. Are characters **stereotyped** in ways listed below?

Male Stereotypes
savage, bloodthirsty "native"
stoic, loyal follower
drunken, mean thief
drunken comic
hunter, tracker
noble child of nature
wise old chief
evil medicine man
brave boy, endowed by nature with special "Indian" qualities

Female Stereotypes
Heavyset, workhorse "squaw"
"Indian princess" (depicted with European features and often in love with a white man for whom she is willing to sacrifice her life)

Occupational Stereotypes
hunters
cattle thieves
warriors
unemployed loafers
craftspeople

2. Does the **story line** create negative characterization of Native Peoples?

A. Are problems confronted and solved by Native Americans, or by kindly white people?

B. Does the text imply that the Native American culture and values are unsuited to a modern, technological society? Or does it suggest that U.S. society might learn from Native Peoples' values and belief systems?

C. Are the Indian characters respected on their own terms? Or must they "prove" themselves by self-sacrifice for whites, or by extraordinary patience or brave deeds?

D. Are Native Americans portrayed as maliciously attacking white settlers and showing a disregard for human life?

E. Are Native Americans presented as mythical human beings, appearing mostly in situations of the past? (Many white children have the impression that Indians are no longer around today.)

F. If the story is about a contemporary Native American child, are the feelings and/or events engendered by living in a racist society included in the text?

G. If a "realistic" story takes place in the present, are the particular oppressive conditions actually endured by Native Peoples today authentically described (e.g., problems of unemployment, violations of fishing rights, police brutality, etc.)? Are the Native People shown struggling to change conditions?

H. If the story is about white children or animals, do they don feathers, whoop and jump, and "play Indian"? (This is a recurrent theme which objectifies and dehumanizes "Indians.")

I. In an alphabet or counting book, are "Indians" the only human beings mixed with animals or objects (e.g., "Nine foolish hens, Ten red Indians" or "I is for ice cream, ink, and Indian")?

3. Do white perspectives negatively characterize the Native American characters?

A. Given the historic period in which the story is set, are the events described so that young white readers understand the Native People's perspective and perceive the Native People as fully human as the white characters?

II LANGUAGE AND TERMINOLOGY

1. Are full names of Native American characters given? Or are they labelled "the Indian," "Injun Joe," etc.? If Indian names are unlike EuroAmerican names, are they presented as English translations of names that have significance in their own language? Or are they mocked or treated "humorously" (e.g., "Chief Five Cents," "Brave Two Nose")? Best of all is to phonetically present the correct Indian name as it is pronounced in its own particular language, e.g., Totanka Iotanka, rather than Sitting Bull, Tashunka Witko, rather than Crazy Horse.

2. Do Native Americans grunt, whoop, or "how" their way through the textbook? Is their speech mocked in any way?

3. Is exotic or stilted speech used (e.g., many moons ago, me come)?

4. Are derogatory words such as *buck, squaw, papoose,* used, instead of, respectively, *man, woman, baby*? Are derogatory terms such as *half-blood, full-blood,* or *mixed-blood* used?

5. Are "loaded words" used (e.g., *savage, stealthy, skulking, stoic, roaming, massacre*—a "massacre" is when Indians win, when whites win it's a "victory"— *heathen, primitive, painted, naked, wild, furtive*)?

6. Are Native Americans compared to animals (e.g., "eyes like a baby fox," "thievish as monkeys," "untamed as a wolf")?

7. Are Native Peoples labelled as either "friendly" or "unfriendly"?

III HISTORICAL ACCURACY

1. Are the sites, dates, actions, and statements about treaties presented accurately? Is the Native perspective included? (The section of this book on U.S. History Texts, pp. 86-103, may be useful.)

Chief Joseph, 1832-1904, a fighting leader of the Nez Perce people, is much more a hero to Native Peoples than is Squanto or other textbook Indian favorites.

2. If the story takes place in the past, is it accurate and particular to one of the hundreds of differing Native cultures in existence at the time?

3. Are achievements of Native Americans (e.g., domestication of corn) presented in context of the benefits accruing to their own societies? Or are these achievements defined solely in terms of their benefits to white people?

4. Are the contributions of Native nations to U.S. law, medicine, philosophy, sports, and literature indicated?

5. Is resistance by Native Peoples to invasion, treaty breaking, acculturation, etc., described? Or is the oppression that resulted in the resistance omitted or glossed over?

6. If Native American heros are described, are those who were hostile to whites also included? Or are the heros selected only those known to have been friendly and helpful to whites (e.g., Pocahontas, Sascatchewea, Squanto)?

IV CULTURAL AUTHENTICITY

1. Does the text present native cultures from a Eurocentric perspective? Or is the culture respectfully presented in terms of the values and belief systems which undergird it?

2. Are totally different Native cultures, lifestyles, clothing, and homes jumbled into one "Indian" stereotype of feathered headdresses, tipis, and peacepipes? Or does the textbook reflect the fact that the hundreds of Native cultures were, and are, enormously diverse?

3. When the text depicts peacepipes, eagle feathers, dances, and ceremonies, are they shown as exotica? Or are their religious significance and cultural usage accurately portrayed?

V ILLUSTRATIONS

1. Are all Native Peoples (of the past) identified by feathers and tipis? Or are the varied clothing, hairstyles, and homes accurate for the particular nation and historical period illustrated?

2. Are Native People (of the present) depicted as wearing feathers, braids, or beads? Or are they illustrated in the many hairstyles and clothes they actually wear (which are generally the same type of contemporary clothing worn by non-native people)?

3. Is an unreal red tone used to show skin color?

4. Do offensive images appear of non-Native American children wearing feathers and "playing Indian"? (If a child dresses as a cowboy or cowgirl, a clown, a police officer, etc., those are professions which go along with a certain outfit. A person of any race can play that professional role. Being an "Indian" is not a profession, but a condition of being. To let children think that feathers or tomahawks symbolize "Indianhood" is to encourage stereotyping and dehumanizing Native Peoples.)

Handicapism In Basal Readers

(credit note: This section is based on a Council study of the stereotypes of disabled people found in children's books and learning materials. For availability of the study, see p. 104.)

HANDICAPISM IS: any attitude, action, or institutional practice which subordinates people based upon their disability.

HANDICAPISM IS EVIDENCED IN U.S. SOCIETY BY: the economic and social oppression of disabled people. One in every six people in the United States has a physical or developmental disability. For children, the number is one in ten (and minority children are overrepresented in this group due to poor prenatal care and later health problems related to poverty). Most of these children can be educated to become self-supporting—*if* sufficient funds were used for that purpose, *if* suitable transportation and access were made available, and *if* employers were educated to hire disabled persons. But none of those "ifs" is happening. Sixty-five per cent of disabled people who want to work cannot, because of employer bias and/or lack of transportation. For those who do find work, earnings—when compared to earnings of non-disabled white males—range from 60 per cent for disabled white males down to 25 per cent for disabled Black females. (That is because racism and sexism, added to handicapism, triply compound the oppression.) The disabled population living below the poverty level is 36 per cent, as against 20 per cent for the general population.

In addition to economic oppression, disabled people are stared at, harassed, and insulted. Despite recent legislation, only 50 per cent of educable disabled children receive an adequate education, and only 20 per cent of job complaints filed by disabled people are acted upon.

EDUCATION HELPS MAINTAIN HANDICAPISM BY: not teaching about the inequities imposed on disabled people, or pointing out the stereotypes and bias against people with disabilities which appear on TV and in books. By this omission educators inadvertently reinforce biased attitudes which, in turn, help to maintain handicapism.

TEXTBOOKS SHOULD: provide accurate information on the specific abilities, as well as disabilities, of people with various physical or mental conditions. They can present fictional and true stories and pictures of disabled children and adults, showing them as fully rounded, interesting people whose disability is merely one aspect of their lives.

A HANDICAPIST TEXTBOOK IS: one that reinforces stereotypes and bias and makes disabled children feel inferior, while encouraging non-disabled children to feel that they, their minds, capabilities, and characters are superior and more deserving of friendship, education, and recreation. Textbooks do this quantitatively—by underrepresenting disabled people—and qualitatively—in the following ways.

The poster above, from the Center for Human Policies, comments on the March of Dimes and connotes a new activism in the field of disability rights.

THREE TEXTBOOK AREAS TO EXAMINE FOR HANDICAPISM—AND MANY QUESTIONS TO PONDER

I CHARACTERIZATION

1. Does the textbook **stereotype** disabled people?

Male Stereotypes

evil blind man with unnatural powers
village "idiot"
evil "peg-leg" or "hook-arm"
pitiful paraplegic
ugly "hunchback"
happy "moron"
deaf and "dumb" sad character
super-"cripple"
pitiful, little "cripple"
childlike dwarf
"insane" criminal
one-eyed pirate
"hard of hearing" crank

Female Stereotypes

"hunchbacked" old crone
blind witch
pitiful blind girl
pitiful, little "cripple"
sexless sad creature
victim of violence
evil witch with a cane
self-pitying whiner

The stereotype above is ageist and sexist, as well as handicapist.

2. Does the text reinforce **occupational stereotypes** about disabled people? (While it is true that there are some disabled people who are forced to beg for a livelihood, who are a burden on their family, or who do not work at all, much of the reason rests with bias in our society. Texts should portray disabled people working at a variety of occupations. In addition, texts should describe the various forms of bias and difficulties which exclude so many disabled people from productive work.

3. Does the textbook have **stereotypic story lines?** The following are examples of story lines which characterize disabled people in negative ways:

   A. Are disabled people always shown as lonesome, unhappy, somehow in need of help from non-disabled children or adults? Is the situation ever vice versa? (Disabled people should be depicted as equals, not as objects of charity—a dehumanizing characterization.)

   B. Is the emphasis placed on what disabled people cannot do, rather than on the wide range of things they can do? (Portrayals of disabled people should show them as productive members of society, as important family members, as students, teachers, workers, etc.)

   C. Are disabled people characterized in the story as possessing individual and complex personalities and interacting with non-disabled story characters based on their individuality, not on their disability? (Disabled people should be depicted in the same situations of love, hate, etc. as are non-disabled characters.)

   D. Does the story line use a disabled person for reasons of sensationalism, as a ploy to create fear, laughter, pity, or curiosity? (They should be depicted as part of an average population, in background as well as in central roles. Story lines which do otherwise, or which depict disabled people only as victims of violence, merely reinforce stereotypes.)

E. Does the story line or the presentation offer accurate information about the various physical and mental disabilities, so that young readers understand exactly how they do, and how they do not, limit the particular disabled person? (Surveys show that adults, as well as children, have gross misconceptions about many physical and mental conditions. In just about all instances, these misconceptions leave the non-disabled public believing that disabled people are much less capable than they actually are.)

F. Does the story line imply a connection between a person's disability and personality? (Messages that make these implications appear in numerous children's "classics" and fairy tales, and since the personality of the disabled character is invariably portrayed as negative, children develop a fear of disabled people.)

G. Does a disabled character perform some super-human feat to be accepted by the non-disabled characters? (Superhuman powers are often attributed to disabled people. Again, such characterization makes the person less, not more, human to young readers. While some blind people, for example, do develop their sense of hearing to a special extent—many do not. Such misleading information should not appear in textbooks.)

H. Does the plot suggest that disabled persons will be happy once they learn to accept their disability and stop pitying themselves? Or is unhappiness shown as being legitimate and often due to society's lack of responsibility for eliminating barriers to education, transportation, work, and recreation?

I. Does the textbook offer positive role models to disabled children of both sexes and all races? (Obviously, no one text can fit in every role model for every category of student. But through stories, illustrations, etc., attempts should be made to be as inclusive as feasible.)

4. Does the author's **perspective** result in a stereotypic characterization? (Very few stories or textbooks are written *by* disabled people. They are almost always written *about* disabled people, e.g., "my deaf sister," or "the blind soldier." This creates many problems. First, to be seen always as an object, rather than the reporter, gives a perspective which cannot be wholly valid. It also limits the humanity of the person who is merely "object." A disabled person's perspective includes many insights not possible for people who do not experience the situation from a similar vantage point. The problem is similar to observing members of a cultural group different from one's own and then writing stories about them. Those stories would rarely ring true to the culture described.)

This book, published by Addison Wesley and based on a TV program about disabilities, is a good classroom resource.

II LANGUAGE AND TERMINOLOGY

(credit note: The section below, called "The Language of Disability" is from the special issue on "Handicapism" in the Council's publication, the Bulletin.*)*

Society's misconceptions about people with disabilities are reinforced by negative, handicapist terms—terms like "cripple," "spastic," "idiot." Continued use of these words contributes to the negative self-images of disabled people and perpetuates handicapist attitudes and practices.

Try to avoid all terms that dehumanize or objectify disabled persons, all terms that characterize disabled persons as dependent or pitiable, all terms that

A common scene since mainstreaming began is shown in this illustration from *Howie Helps Himself,* by Joan Fassler. Art is by Joe Lasker.

perpetuate the myth that disabled persons are incapable of participating in the life of a community.

There is considerable controversy about some terms. The word "handicap" is rejected by many disability rights activists because of its historic associations with a "cap-in-hand," begging image. However, it is still the preferred term of the federal government and is the terminology used in the new legislation to protect disabled people against discrimination. The term "exceptional" has been favored for a number of years by some advocacy groups—for example, the Council for Exceptional Children in Reston, Virginia, and *Exceptional Parent,* a journal published in Massachusetts for parents of disabled children. Many disability activists consider this a euphemism. Massachusetts has a law—Chapter 766—that prohibits labeling of any kind. Children with disabilities in Massachusetts are to be identified only as "children with special needs." The Massachusetts law is considered to be progressive, but there is some criticism that it gives legitimacy to a phrase that emphasizes a person's "neediness."

We have selected the word "disability" as a positive reference to physical or developmental conditions, but we have used "handicapism" because of its negative connotations to describe society's oppression of disabled people.

Below are examples of terminology which, in the light of the new awareness, are considered to be offensive. Preferred substitutes are listed to the right. Some of these terms may appear awkward when first used, but groups using them find that they become readily acceptable after a short while.

Offensive	Preferred
handicap, handicapped person	disability, disabled person
deaf and dumb, deaf-mute, the deaf	deaf, hearing disability, hearing impairment, deaf person
mongoloid	Down's syndrome
cripple, crippled	orthopedic disability, mobility impaired, disabled person
the blind	blind person, sight disability, visually impaired
retard, retardate, idiot, imbecile, feebleminded	retarded, mental impairment, mentally disabled
crazy, maniac, insane, mentally ill	emotional disability, emotional impairment, developmentally disabled

RELATED TERMS TO AVOID: The Minnesota 1976 Governors Conference on Handicapped Individuals proposed that the following entries be deleted from library catalogs: Abnormal children; Abnormalities, Human; Atypical children; Children, Backward; Children, Retarded; Children, Feeble-Minded.

III ILLUSTRATIONS

1. In group scenes, are one or more disabled people included in the play, work, or general activity (e.g., people on crutches or in wheelchairs, people with hearing aids, people with Down's Syndrome, etc.)?

2. Are disabled people illustrated with as much personality and individuality as non-disabled characters?

3. In basal readers, are disabled people approximately 10 per cent of those illustrated?

Ageism In Basal Readers

(credit note: This section is based on a study of 656 children's books by Edward F. Ansello reported in the Council's publication, the Bulletin. *For availability of the study, see p. 104.)*

AGEISM IS: any attitude, action, or institutional practice which subordinates people based on their age. (While ageism is defined as discrimination based upon age and is also used against young people, this section deals only with discrimination against older people.)

AGEISM IS EVIDENCED IN U.S. SOCIETY BY: the oppressive condition of 12 per cent of Americans who are over 65. This percentage is growing rapidly. About 30 per cent work, full *or* part time, though many more are able to work and would like to do so. Average income is pitifully low ($75 per week) and two out of three people with incomes below the poverty line are older citizens. Over 30 per cent live in substandard housing, and 25 percent of all suicides are committed by people in this age range. Since youth is worshipped in U.S. society, older people are made to feel ugly and useless. Like one's race, sex, or disability, one's age is not a matter of choice. It is irrevocable and will eventually affect everybody. Hence ageism is an offense against us all.

EDUCATION HELPS MAINTAIN AGEISM BY: neglecting to challenge the stereotypes and bias in society, thus inadvertently helping to maintain the status quo. Despite the rapidly growing numbers of older people in the U.S. population, fewer and fewer children have direct contact with them. Therefore, most children get their concepts about old age from books and TV. To combat ageist stereotypes, educators could arrange school visits by older people who are actively engaged in the struggle to improve their rights and also discuss with students the stereotypes which appear in books and on TV.

TEXTBOOKS UNDERREPRESENT OLDER PEOPLE BECAUSE: while 12 per cent of U.S. citizens are over 65, only 3.6 per cent of main characters in children's stories are older people. Though they were found, by the study cited above, to make an appearance in 16 per cent of children's books, in only 10 per cent of those times are they portrayed as active or in positive roles. While 55 per cent of the storybook characters in the study are male, in real life only 25 per cent of people over 65 are male. Minorities, especially women, are the most underrepresented. Finally, older people are only 4.5 per cent of the total number of illustrations. While these are statistics about storybooks, any cursory examination of school textbooks will uncover similar failings.

TEXTBOOKS SHOULD: challenge stereotypes and bias by presenting many more accounts—fiction and fact—about the accomplishments and lives of active, older people.

AN AGEIST TEXTBOOK IS: one that stereotypes older people or leads young people to feel that older people's mental and physical capabilities are inevitably inferior, due to their age. Textbooks do this

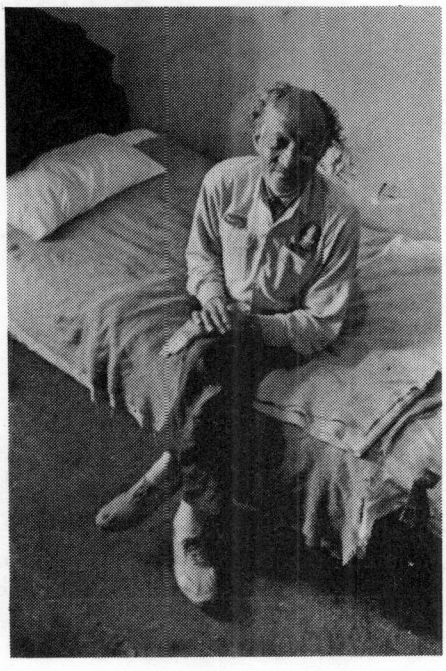

Ira Nowenski's moving photographs in *The Eye of Conscience: photographers and social change* (by Milton Meltzer and Bernard Cole) point out the all-too-common connection between poverty and age.

quantitatively—by underrepresenting older people—or they do it qualitatively—in the following ways.

THREE TEXTBOOK AREAS TO EXAMINE FOR AGEISM— AND MANY QUESTIONS TO PONDER

I CHARACTERIZATION

1. Does the textbook **stereotype** people according to their age?

Male Stereotypes	**Female Stereotypes**
hard of hearing	rocking in a chair
walking with a cane	boring and old fashioned
forgetful	frumpily clothed
rocking in a chair	stubborn
blank faced with bent body	meddling in family affairs
wearing baggy clothes	asexual
asexual	knitting all day
cruel and frightening	ugly old shrew
all wise and patient	wicked witch
	sad and helpless

2. Does the text reinforce the stereotype that older people have **no occupations or useful role** in life? Textbooks should make it clear to children that many older people do work, and that many more would work if not for employer bias, forced retirement, or other forms of discrimination. While it is true that many older people are lonely and unhappy, the reasons are often tied to poverty, rather than to age. To characterize older people—as a group—as sad and useless, is to reinforce stereotypes.

3. Does the textbook have **stereotypic story lines?** For example:
   A. Is a short, idyllic relationship between a child and an older person interrupted by death? (While death is inevitable, equating death and age is inadvisable.)

   B. Is the story about an older person who is unhappy until a child intervenes and plays or spends time with her or him? (Again, this is dehumanizing and certainly would not be a story line about a younger adult and a child.)

   C. Does the older character have simply a "walk-on" role as someone frightening, funny, sad? (This, too, reinforces stereotypes.)

   D. Are age integrated activities and friendships portrayed? (If not, the text is subtly deprecating the goal of people accepting each other because of their human qualities, not because of their age.)

   E. Does the text portray older people only as decrepit grandparents? (Most people become grandparents in their late forties or early fifties and are quite hale and hearty while their grandchildren are growing up.)

   F. Do the stories omit information about the particular problems and needs of older people? Is information provided about fixed incomes in inflationary times? About the limited lives circumscribed by poverty? About the pain of being stigmatized because of age? (Omission of such information in stories and textbooks can reinforce

When older people to do turn up in children's stories, they frequently look like this hard-of-hearing, decrepit-looking stereotype.

stereotypes and thus assure the repetition of mistreatment of older people. To achieve a humane society, textbooks must help to develop knowing and caring young people.)

4. Does the **author's perspective** result in stereotypic characterizations?
   A. Is the perspective always that of a child observing the older people? Or does the viewpoint of the older characters sometimes emerge? (When people's viewpoints and concerns are omitted, their full humanity is diminished.)
   B. Does the author's own fear or distaste of old age surface? (Many books instill fear of older people into children by ascribing such fears to the young protagonists. Actually, most young children are not afraid of, or bored with, older people based on their own limited experiences. It is often the perspective of the author that develops such attitudes in young people.)
   C. Is the perspective of other cultures which show marked respect for older people included in the textbook?

This non-ageist book presents a grandmother who is a vital, interesting character.

II LANGUAGE AND TERMINOLOGY

1. Does the textbook use dehumanizing, limited word description of older people? (Over 74 per cent of all physical descriptions of older people in the study of 656 children's books consisted of the single adjective *old*. Another 5.4 per cent consisted of the word *little*. 4.2 per cent of *elder*, 1.6 per cent of *small*, and 2.0 per cent of *ancient*. These five words comprise almost five-sixths of all physical descriptors applied in the books. Personality descriptors were *sad* and *poor*—24 per cent.)

2. Does the text omit names of older characters, simply calling them "The old woman," "Old man," etc.?

3. Are derogatory statements such as, "You can't teach an old dog new tricks," or "There's no fool like an old fool," included in the text?

4. Are euphemisms used which avoid the reality of old age? (Phrases like *senior citizen, golden years,* etc. are seen by some activists, like the *Gray Panthers,* to be patronizing—an avoidance of the reality of old age.)

III ILLUSTRATIONS

1. In group scenes, are older people included when they could logically appear?

2. Are the older people illustrated without stereotypic props such as canes, bent bodies, sagging clothes, rocking chairs?

3. Are the older people illustrated as possessing personality and variety?

More Problems In Textbooks

MATERIALISM

Because children, like other consumers, are bombarded with sophisticated hard-sell of material goods, they are conditioned to believe that material accumulation is life's primary goal. Books should counteract this materialistic pressure if we are to achieve a society with meaningful human values.

1. Does the story imply that possession of consumer goods or wealth is the basis for valuing people or valuing oneself?

2. Is there an implication that happiness is achieved through the accumulation of possessions?

3. Is there an implication that those people who have a great deal of material possessions are somehow more worthy than people who do not? (The real danger of this outlook is that poor people are blamed for their own poverty.)

4. When stories are about other countries, is there an implication that material wealth and industrialization are essential to achieve "civilization"?

COMPETITION

While ours is a competitive society, some people still choose to live in cooperative lifestyles. So that children can consciously make their own choices, it is important that they learn that competition is *not* a result of human nature but stems from cultural conditioning. Many Native American cultures are cooperative (as are some other cultures throughout the world), and sharing and cooperating with others in the community can be an alternative way of life.

1. Are children made to feel that being "first" or "best" is worth using "any means necessary" to get there? Or are they helped to understand that competition is a suitable approach in certain situations and that cooperation is often a more suitable approach?

ELITISM

Much of children's literature sends out snobbish messages about some people being inferior to others based upon their lower job status, their lifestyle, their personal mannerisms or "poor" taste.

1. Are characters presented as valuable for their basic qualities (kindness, alertness, etc.), or are they valued for external mannerisms (speech, taste in clothing, etc.)?

CLASSISM

(credit note: The ideas in the section which follows are from a study by Judith Woodruff, to be published in the Bulletin *under the title of "The World of Work in Children's Books." See p. 104 for availability.)*

Traditional English novels and many fairy tales imply that royalty or people of the "upper classes" are naturally superior to common folk, servants or working people. While this is not commonplace in stories and learning materials of today, a spin-off of such classism *is* important today—the utter invisibility of working people and the world of work in children's literature and basal readers.

Classism in texts is primarily a problem of omission. It's not that work and workers are directly treated in a put-down fashion. Rather they are treated as mere window-dressing and not as essential to life and all human endeavor. (Of course, in history textbooks, overt acts of classist commission occur frequently, in stereotypes and distortions about labor history, for example.) What is needed is a greater knowledge about, and respect for, all types of work. A study of occupational interest among students in Illinois showed that 95 per cent of the elementary school children wanted to be professionals, although fewer than 12 per cent of all workers in the United States are in that category. The children also showed extremely elitist responses in their occupational preferences.

Questions to be considered in evaluating basal readers and other textbooks follow. Of course, all of the points mentioned need not appear in every textbook. But they include thoughts to consider in aiming for meaningful curriculum materials.

1. Do the textbooks include stories in which workers are primary characters? (We are excluding "window-dressing" characters like "the friendly policeman.")

2. Are the worker's feelings about working conditions, the work process, her/his relationship to other workers, his/her relationship to management, and the relationship of the work day to her/his family life portrayed? Is the worker presented as a fully human character?

3. Are the people required to run an institution adequately represented? (For example, in educational material about hospitals, do children learn of janitors and cooks as well as of doctors and nurses?)

4. Does the material clarify the reasons people work (for both economic reasons and reasons of self-fulfillment)?

5. Are unemployment and its impact on family life portrayed?

6. Are negative value judgments implied about the status of particular kinds of work?

7. Are the role and importance of common working people in shaping history presented?

The Influence Of Textbooks

(credit note: The information in this section was taken from a report by Jeana Wirtenberg, of the National Institute of Education, and from a paper by Patricia B. Campbell, of William Paterson College.)

Hillel Black, in *The American School Book,* estimates that 75 per cent of a child's classwork and 90 per cent of the homework focuses on the textbooks. From elementary through high school, a child reads at least 32,000 textbook pages. The Association of American Publishers has noted:

> Textbooks play an important part in education, transmitting not only facts and figures, but ideas and cultural values. The words and pictures children see in school influence the development of the attitudes they carry into adult life: these words and pictures not only express ideas, but are part of the educational experience which shapes ideas.

Just how influential are textbooks in shaping ideas? A rundown of research shows that children's attitudes towards another person's race, ethnicity, gender, social class or age can be influenced by books. Research also shows that the development of a child's self-esteem, values, inspirations, and fears may be either assisted or inhibited by the content of textbooks. Through identification with characters and situations in textbooks, a child learns to cope with similar situations in everyday life.

Measures of academic achievement also reflect the effects of textbook bias on children. Non-academic aspects of the curriculum determine children's acquisition and maintenance of reading skills, understanding, and retention of subject matter, and their motivation and success in problem-solving abilities.

Futhermore, the preparation that children receive from schoolbooks affects their career interests, expectations, and achievements. Biased curricular materials limit the career options that minorities and females foresee, and textbook bias further impedes their potential development.

The following research studies document the effects of books on children:

Barclay, L.K. "The Emergence of Vocational Expectations in Pre-School Children," *Journal of Vocational Behavior,* (1974) *4,* pp. 1-14.

Deutsch, S. "Disadvantages of Culturally Deprived Children," *Integrated Education,* (Chicago: Rand McNally, 1969), pp. 31-32.

Donlon, T.F., Ekstrom, R., and Lockheed, M. *Performance Consequences of Sex Bias in the Content of Major Achievement Batteries: Final Report,* ERIC Document ED, 151, 415, (July 1977).

Fisher, F.L. "The Influences of Reading and Discussion on the Attitudes of Fifth Graders Toward American Indians," (unpublished Ph.D. dissertation, University of California, Berkeley, 1965).

Fischer, P.L., and Torney, J.V. "Influence of Children's Stories on Dependency, a Sex-Typed Behavior," *Developmental Psychology*, (1976) *12*, pp. 489-90.

Flerx, V.C., Fidler, D.S., and Rogers, R.W. "Sex Role Stereotypes: Developmental Aspects and Early Intervention," *Child Development*, (1976) *47*, pp. 998-1007.

Georgeoff, J.P. "The Effect of the Curriculum Upon the Self-Concept of Children in Racially Integrated Fourth Grade Classrooms," paper to American Educational Research Association (1968).

Gezi, K.I., and Johnson, B. "Enhancing Racial Attitudes Through the Study of Black Heritage," *Childhood Education, 46*, no. 7 (1970), p. 339.

Grambs, J.D. "Sex Stereotypes in Instructional Materials, Literature and Language," *Women's Studies Abstracts*, 1 (4), pp. 1-4 (1972), pp. 91-94.

Hare, B. "Black and White Self-Esteem in Social Science: An Overview," *Journal of Negro Education, 46* (Spring 1977), pp. 141-56.

Hare, B. *Black Girls: A Comparative Analysis of Self-Perception Background by Race, Sex, and Socioeconomic Background* (Johns Hopkins University, 1979).

Jackson, E. "Effects of Reading Upon Attitudes Toward the Negro Race," *Library Quarterly, 14* (January 1944), pp. 47-54.

Jenkins, S. "Sexism in Children's Books and Elementary Classroom Materials," *Sexism in Language* (National Council of Teachers of English, 1977), p. 162.

Johnson, D.W. "The Effects of a Freedom School on Its Students," *The Urban R's: Race Relations as the Problem in Urban Ed.,* (R. Dentler, B. Mackler, eds., Praeger, New York, 1967).

Johnson, E. and Henton, C. "The Relationship Between Self-Concept of Negro Elementary School Children and Their Academic Achievement," Cooperative Project 1592, U.S. Department of H.E.W. (1964).

Litcher, J.H., and Johnson, D.W. "Changes in Attitudes toward Negroes of White Elementary School Students After Use of Multiethnic Readers," *Journal of Educational Psychology,* (1969) *60*, pp. 148-52.

Metz, S.S. "The Relationship of Age and Sex of Four, Five and Six Year Olds to the Perceptions of Sex Roles as Portrayed in Children's Literature," ERIC Document ED 097124, (August, 1974).

Milton, G.A. "The Effects of Sex-Role Identification Upon Problem-Solving Skill," *Journal of Abnormal Psychology, 55* (1957), pp. 208-12.

Narang, H.L. "Improving Reading Ability of Indian Children," *Elementary English,* (February, 1974), pp. 191-92.

Poussaint, A. U.S. Commission on Civil Rights, *What Students Perceive* (Clearinghouse Publication 24, 1970).

Ruth, R.W. "The Effects of Black Studies on Negro Fifth Grade Students," *Journal of Negro Education, 38* (Fall 1969), pp. 435-39.

Sandberg, B. and White, M.A. "The Effect of Sex-Role Modeling on Occupational Interests of Children," paper at 86th Convention of American Psychological Association, Toronto, (1978).

Schau, C.G., Kahn, L., and Tremaine, L. "The Effects of Stories on Elementary School Children's Gender-Stereotyped Attitudes Toward Adult Occupations," (unpublished manuscript, University of New Mexico, Albuquerque, 1978).

Schau, C.G., "Evaluating the Use of Sex Role Reversed Stories for Changing Children's Stereotypes," (Paper to the American Educational Research Association, Toronto, 1978).

Scott, K.P. "Elementary Pupils' Perceptions of Reading and Social Studies Materials: Does the Sex of the Main Character Make a Difference?" (Dissertation Abstracts UMI 780973, Ann Arbor, Michigan, 1977).

Smith, N.B. "Some Effects of Reading in Children," *Elementary English,* (1948), pp. 271-78.

Stotsky, W. "Intervention In Sex Role Socialization," *Women's Studies Newsletter, 4,* (1976), pp. 6-7.

Tauran, R.H. "The Influences of Reading on the Attitudes of Third Graders Towards Eskimos," (unpublished Ph.D. dissertation, University of Maryland, College Park, 1967).

Thompson, H. *Education for Cross Cultural Enrichment,* U.S. Dept. of Interior, Bureau of Indian Affairs (1964).

Westphal, R. *The Effects of a Primary-Grade Level Inter and Ethnic Curriculum on Racial Prejudice,* R and E Research Associates, San Francisco, (1977).

Whipple, G. *Appraisal of the City Schools' Reading Program,* Division of Improvement of Instruction, Detroit, Michigan, (1963).

Yee, A. H. and Fruth, M.J. "Do Black Studies Make a Difference in Ghetto Children's Achievement and Attitudes?" *Journal of Negro Education, 42* (1971), p. 33.

California Criteria For The Evaluation Of Instructional Materials

(credit note: The following are excerpted from the guidelines for members of the State of California's Legal Compliance Committee. Many other states have similar guidelines.)

I. Male and Female Roles—*Ed. Code 9240(a), 9243(a)*

In order to encourage the individual development and self-esteem of each child, regardless of gender, instructional materials, when they portray people (or animals having identifiable human attributes), shall portray women and men, girls and boys, in a wide variety of occupational, emotional, and behavioral situations, presenting both sexes in the full range of their human potential.

1. Descriptions, depictions, labels, or retorts which tend to demean, stereotype, or be patronizing toward females must not appear.

(Do references to women indicate that their talents, intelligence, or activities are inferior to those of men? Or that they are incapable of handling a situation without a man's assistance? For example, there should be no labels such as "old maids," "fishwives," "henpeckers," or "woman driver," or retorts such as "she's only a girl" or "what do you expect from a girl?" Such references constitute adverse reflections.)

2. Instructional materials that generally or incidentally reflect contemporary American society, regardless of the subject area, must contain references to, or illustrations of, males and females approximately evenly, except as limited by accuracy.

3. Mentally and physically active, creative, problem-solving roles, and success and failure in those roles, should be divided approximately evenly between male and female characters.

(The consequences of activity undertaken by males and females must be observed. Positive or negative results can come from the undertaking of any task. A pattern of positive or negative results, most simply defined as success or failure, should not emerge as correlated with sex. It is not suggested that all characters succeed at all times. However, the ratio of success to failure must be approximately the same for female characters as for male characters.)

4. Emotions—for example, fear, anger, aggression, excitement, or tenderness—should occur randomly among characters regardless of gender.

5. Traditional activities engaged in by characters of one sex should be balanced by the presentation of nontraditional activities for characters of that sex.

6. If professional or executive roles, or vocations, trades, or other gainful occupations are portrayed, men and women should be represented therein approximately equally.

Helen Simpson was one of the first female pilots. Information like this should be presented to children.

7. Where lifestyle choices are discussed, boys and girls should be offered an equally wide range of such aspirations and choices.

(Various occupations and various lifestyles—marriage, remaining single, raising children or not doing so—should also be cast in an affirmative light.)

8. Whenever a material presents developments in history or current events, or achievements in art, science, or any other field, the contributions of women should be included and discussed when historically accurate.

9. Imbalance or inequality of any kind, when presented for historical accuracy, should, in the student edition of the instructional material, be interpreted in light of contemporary standards and circumstances.

10. Sexually neutral language—for example, "people," "persons," "men and women," "pioneers," "they"—should generally be used.

II. Ethnic and Cultural Groups—*Ed. Code 9240(b) and 9243(a)*

In order to project the cultural diversity of our society, instill in each child a sense of pride in his or her heritage, eradicate the seeds of prejudice, and encourage the individual development of each child, instructional materials, when portraying people (or animals having identifiable human attributes), shall include a fair representation of majority and minority group characters portrayed in a wide variety of occupational and behavioral roles, and present the contributions of ethnic and cultural groups, thereby reinforcing the self-esteem and potential of all people and helping the members of minority groups to find their rightful place in our society.

1. Descriptions, depictions, or labels which tend to demean, stereotype, or be patronizing toward minority groups must not appear.

2. When diverse ethnic or cultural groups are portrayed, such portrayal must not depict differences in customs or lifestyle as undesirable and must not reflect an adverse value judgment of such differences.

3. Instructional materials that generally or incidentally reflect contemporary American society, regardless of the subject area, must contain references to, or illustrations of, a fair proportion of diverse ethnic groups.

4. Mentally active, creative, and problem-solving roles, and success and failure in those roles, should be divided in fair proportion between majority and minority group characters.

>(It is necessary to look to the consequences of activities undertaken by majority and minority group characters presented in the material. Positive or negative results, success or failure, can flow from the undertaking of any tasks, and it is not suggested that all characters succeed at all times. A pattern of success or failure, however, should not emerge as correlated with the race, ethnicity, or cultural background of the character.)

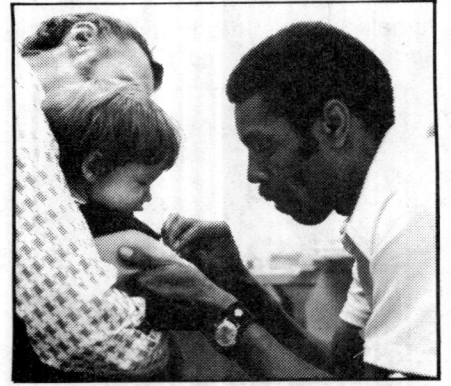

5. The portrayal of minority characters in roles to which they have been traditionally restricted by society should be balanced by the presentation of nontraditional activities for characters of that race.

6. Minority persons should be depicted in the same range of socioeconomic settings as are persons of the majority group.

7. Depiction of diverse ethnic and cultural groups should not be limited to the root culture, but rather expanded to include such groups within the mainstream of American life.

8. If professional or executive roles, or vocations, trades, or other gainful occupations are portrayed, majority and minority groups should be presented therein in fair proportion.

>(Although no specific number of percentage for each statutorily noted minority group is specified, "tokenism" for any minority group is as unacceptable in instructional materials as it is in the real world of employment.)

9. Whenever developments in history or current events, or achievements in art, science, or any other field are presented, the contributions of minority peoples, and particularly the identification of prominent minority persons, should be included and discussed when historically accurate.

10. Imbalance or inequality of any kind, when presented for historical accuracy,

should, in the student edition of the instructional materials, be interpreted in light of contemporary standards and circumstances.

In order to portray accurately the cultural and racial diversity and the male and female roles in our society, instructional materials must encourage students to understand not only the historical roles and contributions of women and minorities but also *the forces which shaped those roles and contributions and how and why the contemporary roles and contributions of women and minorities are different.*

Guidelines for Evaluation of Instructional Materials

California State Board of Education, September 12, 1974

Checklist For Basal Readers

This checklist cannot be used without a clear understanding of the content of pages 30 to 72. It is much more rewarding to work in teams when analyzing basal readers, as the process is time consuming and requires inevitable value judgements.

ILLUSTRATIONS:

	Males								Females							
	White	Black	Latino	Asian American	Native American	Older	Disabled	Total	White	Black	Latino	Asian American	Native American	Older	Disabled	Total
Number of People																
Number of Central Characters																
Number of Positive Images																
Number of Negative Images																

	Only Males	Mainly Males	Mixed	Mainly Females	Only Females
Number of Pages Showing					

	Males			Females		
	White	Minority	Total	White	Minority	Total
Number of Occupations						

	High Activity		Moderate Activity		Passivity	
	Male	Female	Male	Female	Male	Female
Number people Active/Passive						

PRINT MATTER:

	Males								Females							
	White	Black	Latino	Asian American	Native American	Older	Disabled	Total	White	Black	Latino	Asian American	Native American	Older	Disabled	Total
Number of pages on which:																
Main characters are																
Stereotypes are of																
Good role models of																

Number of Times:	Sexist	Racist	Ageist	Handicapist
Language Offensive				
Perspective Biased				
Story Line Stereotypic				
Omissions Create Bias				
Culturally Inauthentic				

1. Does each grade level reader show some variety in lifestyles? Some nurturant, sensitive males? Some independent females?

2. Does each provide some insights into problems of discrimination in our society?

3. Does each provide some role models who act to end social inequities?

4. Does the teacher's manual offer ways to use the reading material to develop student analytic skills and to raise their awareness of equity issues?

Checklist For Literature Anthologies

(credit note: The following section is adapted from an unpublished manuscript entitled Presenting People *authored by the editorial personnel at Scott, Foresman & Company.)*

Literature plays an important role in defining values and interpreting reality, and such definitions and interpretations are transmitted to the adolescents who read literature anthologies. A number of studies to examine the impact of reading content on changing attitudes have revealed the following: positive character presentations influence student attitudes to change in a positive direction; negative character presentations influence attitudes to change in a negative direction.

Many classics considered part of the traditional literary fare have conveyed negative attitudes that are racist, sexist, etc. To completely eliminate these works from the curriculum, however, would be unwise, if they possess literary merit, appeal to students, and portray the social and cultural influences that have affected people of a particular era.

A multicultural California-based task force examining instructional materials had this to say:

Some people become upset when the works of persons whom they greatly admire and respect are shown to be biased or racist. In their unwavering devotion to such writers, some people fail to acknowledge the fact that writers are human, possessing the same frailties as others and subject to the prevailing sociologic forces of their time. Moreover, such "revelations" should not detract from the literary contributions those persons have made. It should be recognized, when applicable, that some such authors were ahead of their time, albeit not up to measure—using today's standards.

The questions which must be satisfactorily answered in terms of biased sexist and racist inclusions in literature are the following:

Is there assurance that students will be provided with sufficient background in order that they will be able to understand the author's perspective and the historicity of the inclusion?

Are the children sufficiently mature to understand the historical context of the biased or racist inclusion?

How will students regard persons in the classroom or in society whose group is portrayed?

While every effort must be made to find and include works of quality that are unbiased, those works that contain biases and stereotypes can be dealt with constructively. In "Why a Feminist Approach to Literature?" Nancy Topping Bazin has observed that literature "reflects the culture and the ideology of the society that produced it. If we teach literature or any other work without challenging the ideology inherent in that work, then we are encouraging the continuance of the status quo," and further, that an analytical approach to literature can enable students to "discover what kind of society they want to create and what the obstacles are to its creation."

While Jo, the main "little woman" was a "tomboy," the sexist message in this classic is that girls must eventually grow up and conform to "feminine" roles. Many classroom discussions can be planned around this book, and other sexist or racist books for older children.

1. Does the anthology give adequate representation to literary works by members of racial minorities and by women of all races?

(There should be a concerted effort to find fresh, new representative works by women and third world authors, rather than simply to rely on the same standard fare of "proven" works by "acceptable" authors.)

2. Do the selections represent minority groups in a diverse, sensitive, and culturally authentic manner?

(This kind of accuracy depends first, on diligent scholarship by the editors and, second, on a willingness to seek out and enlist third world authors and consultants for input on perspective and authenticity.)

3. Do some of the selections include a feminist perspective?

(Works by women active in the feminist movement over the last 150 years provide a rich source of literature.)

4. Do the selections include accounts of the lives of ordinary working men and women?

5. Do editorial comments provide relevant historical, cultural, or social background about the oppression experienced by minority people and women? Do they connect this oppression with the fact that relatively few works by women and third world people were written or published?

6. Do editorial comments encourage the class discussion of stereotypes and bias wherever these occur in the selections?

7. When presenting literary history, is due recognition given to the literary achievements of women and minorities?

(It is important for young people to know, for example, that women played a major part in the development of the novel form; that African heritage had a molding impact on U.S. literature and music; that Black writers have had considerable influence on modern poetry; that many anonymous literary works may have had women authors; etc.)

8. When females and third world people appear as characters in a story, are they sometimes major, strong, admirable individuals? Or are they always relegated to subordinate, passive, or undignified roles?

9. Is there an attempt to portray, without condescension, some values, cultures, or lifestyles other than those of a white, middle-class, male-oriented society?

10. Is the editorial commentary free of biased terminology?

Stories by Japanese American Toshio Mori should be included in high school literature anthologies because they are well written and they explore Japanese American culture.

Checklist For Dictionaries

(credit note: The following section is adapted from an unpublished manuscript entitled Presenting People *authored by the editorial personnel at Scott, Foresman & Company.)*

A good dictionary includes the standard language a reader is likely to encounter. Because a dictionary is descriptive rather than prescriptive, it must reflect language as it is, rather than dictate language as it should or could be. Unlike those who gather materials in other disciplines, the compilers of a dictionary cannot simply eliminate terms that have racist, sexist or other derogatory connotations. When a word in common usage is offensive to members of a group, however, this fact should be made abundantly clear either in its definition or by a specific label. *Hag,* defined as "a very ugly, old woman," is obviously a pejorative term, according to its definition. Other derogatory words whose definitions do not necessarily indicate pejorative meanings should be labeled offensive (e.g., *colored, squaw*).

Given its prescribed material, however, a dictionary can serve to combat racism and sexism in many ways. Aside from those ways specifically mentioned, dictionaries should include entries such as *ageism, Ms., handicapism, racism,* and *sexism* that address themselves to a new awareness of bias.

1. If the dictionary bears a recent copyright, does it include the entries just mentioned?

2. Think of six words that you would consider "active" (*build, fix, run,* etc.). Then think of six words that connote passivity or incompetence (*helpless, incompetent, suffer,* etc.). See how the dictionary defines and illustrates these words.

3. At random, select 25 pictures. List the ratio of females to males. Indicate whether the words illustrated have positive or negative connotations, or if they are neutral. Are members of minority groups represented? Are any racial or sexual sterotypes suggested?

4. Look up 20 words that have traditionally been considered stereotypical or have been associated with a particular group or sex (e.g., *professional, doctor, sew, pot, cheerleader, girlish, afraid, faint, strong, daring, backward, ruthless, underprivileged, ambitious, gossip, massacre, primitive, snoop, inscrutable, coy*) to see if their definitions suggest bias.

5. Are *he, his, him* routinely used to indicate both males *and* females? Do words like *man* and *mankind* appear instead of *human being* and *person?*

6. Are first names and surnames nearly always Anglicized?

7. Check any group of 12 consecutive pages to determine the number of females and males in both the pictures and the copy. Count the words associated with each sex that have negative and positive connotations.

In the best picture dictionary to date (Scott, Foresman), the top illustration is captioned, "She proudly displayed her trophy." The woman above illustrates the word, "clown." The dictionary also shows people of color in positive ways.

8. Check to see if the dictionary attempts to portray "the typical middle-class life" exclusively or to present a white, Eurocentric bias. Find out the following: What holidays are described? How is *immigrant* defined? How are words such as *tribe, native,* or *savage* defined? Do words beginning with *non-* imply a Eurocentric norm (e.g., *non-white*)?

9. Are third world people used in illustrations mainly as "props" for exotic dress (e.g., parkas or grass skirts)? Or are they routinely used to illustrate ordinary activities or objects?

Checklist For Biographies

(credit note: The following section is adapted from an unpublished manuscript entitled Presenting People *authored by the editorial personnel at Scott, Foresman & Company.)*

1. Are works described in terms that reinforce sexual or racial stereotypes?

    (Men as well as women write works whose mood and imagery may be characterized as *delicate, sensitive, fragile,* or *simple,* while both sexes produce writing that is *powerful, influential,* or *authoritative.* The terms *masculine* and *feminine* are unsuitable and meaningless adjectives in describing the works of any author. Use of words such as *primitive* and *exotic* should be carefully analyzed to make sure they do not suggest cultural or racial biases.)

2. Does the biography of a woman omit superfluous details or extraneous comments if their equivalent would not be included in the biography of a man (e.g., physical descriptions, details of dress, marital and parental status)?

3. Does it include details about both parents, if relevant, when providing a subject's family background?

    (Too often a biographical subject is introduced in terms of his or her father's profession, while the mother's name is not even mentioned.)

4. Does the work use titles such as *Ms.* only when *Mr.* would appear when referring to a male author? Is it consistent about the use of first names?

    (If a biography would not call Hemingway *Ernest,* it should not take the liberty of calling Dickinson *Emily* or Brooks *Gwendolyn.*)

5. Does the biography infer that the achievements of women or minority people are unusual in themselves?

    (This inference should be carefully avoided. Watch for key words such as *remarkable, intelligent, inspite of,* or *nevertheless* to make sure they do not convey sexist or racist connotations. E.g., "Despite her frail nature, she wrote powerful verse" or "He was raised in the ghetto; nevertheless he went on to write poetry that captures the beauty of close family relationships.")

6. When the accomplishments of a literary figure were achieved in the face of hostile historical, cultural, or social factors, or whenever such factors influenced a work, is pertinent background information provided?

7. Does the use of qualifiers establish the white, male writer as the norm (e.g., calling Langston Hughes one of America's best-known Black poets or referring to Joyce Carol Oates as a fast-rising woman novelist)?

8. Are the general criteria for nonsexist, nonracist language applied?

This report on textbooks in Kalamazoo, Michigan schools found that of all biographies and biographical items, 75 per cent were about males.

Checklist For Math Textbooks

(credit note: The following section is adapted from an unpublished manuscript entitled Presenting People *authored by the editorial personnel at Scott, Foresman & Company.)*

The purpose of math books is not to tell stories, present philosophies, or create heros. Their intent is to teach numerical processes, and when people are presented at all they are merely vehicles to convey numbers. Whatever their intentions, mathematics textbooks give strong social messages, and their effect has traditionally been to reinforce bias. While girls in math problems have been depicted in passive or sex-stereotyped roles, such as buying three yards of ribbon, members of minority groups have been grossly underrepresented or omitted altogether—suggesting that their intellectual capabilities are limited, at best.

Mathematics problems dominated by a white, male orientation fail to provide a source of identification for minority members and females in general, thus failing to encourage the potential and aptitudes of considerably more than half the students who use math texts.

Newer math texts are changing for the better. However, the old math texts are still very much in use. As with other biased textbooks, we urge educators to devise strategies that will counter the sexism and racism as they use the textbook. The criteria given below may be shared with students for this purpose. In any case, such guidelines should be used in purchasing new mathematics textbooks.

1. Analyze any series of at least 40 story problems. How many times and in what context are females mentioned? Males? Compare the number of females to males in problems dealing with the following: active endeavors, such as building things; money matters; machines; marketing; sports; jobs—traditional and nontraditional; domestic activities; owning or running businesses.

2. Is textual matter free of sexist language (e.g., "the student . . . his," "men of science")?

3. Along with the standard "Mary, Bob, and Jim," are there names such as Leroy, José, and Juanita? Is there a representative number of family names such as Giovanni, Tsun, Lopez, and Baramba?

4. Are there inferences, however unintended, that males are more competent in activities in general and in math in particular, than girls?

5. Do illustrations depict members of minority groups, women in general, disabled and older people, in a variety of roles? Are working people shown as well as professionals?

6. In areas of higher mathematics where books list leaders in the history of mathematics, are the names and pictures of women and third world mathematicians noted?

This booklet on careers, produced by the Lawrence Hall of Science at the University of California, Berkeley, discusses many well paying jobs for women. Unfortunately, most women entering college have insufficient math credits to train for such careers. Sexist math textbooks are one cause.

Checklist For Bilingual Textbooks

(credit note: Much of the following section is based upon studies by Iris Santos Rivera, Director of the National Origin Desegregation Assistance Center in Denver, Colorado.)

A bilingual textbook which is not also a bicultural textbook is subtly beaming this message to students: "The dominant culture is where it's at!" Moreover, many of the textbooks and story books hurriedly devised for bilingual programs are merely translations of previously published English books, glorifying Western culture and values. Rarely are so-called bilingual materials thoughtful presentations of material from and about two cultures.

Most of the limited materials available are in Spanish and English—reflecting the large number of students using Spanish. The material available for students who speak other languages is more circumscribed. In very recent years, some groups of educators, like the Chinese American Teachers' Association, have produced culturally respectful and well done bilingual instructional materials.

While bilingual educators are rejecting textbooks printed in two languages of late, many such materials are still in school use. Whether or not the text is bilingual or in one language other than English, educators should check out the following points.

1. Is the textbook free of sex bias?

(Frequently materials are translation of texts or stories originally published in English at a time when sex stereotyping was more prevalent than today. However, many materials originally written in Spanish and originally published in Spain, Mexico or Latin America are worse. They are extremely sexist—to a degree beyond older materials from the United States.)

2. If stereotyped sexist characters are introduced as reflecting their particular culture, are some other characters of that culture also depicted as struggling to change sexist aspects of their culture?

(No culture is static, and textbooks should make it clear that attitudes towards sex roles are changing the world over. People of either sex are *not* betraying their cultural roots by working to change some attitudes and customs.)

3. Is the textbook culturally authentic?

(Books from Spain often contain irrelevant vocabulary, in addition to being culturally irrelevant to Chicano, Puerto Rican or other Latino children. They also are often religiously biased and solidly middle to upper class in orientation. Many Spanish materials printed in the United States were prepared by Cuban "refugees" in Miami and are not culturally relevant to Puerto Rican or Chicano children. Textbooks used in Puerto Rico and sold for use in the United States are published by a U.S. commercial publisher. These are culturally *neutral*—Dick and Jane in tanface. All of the above have *no* illustrations of

The illustrations in this Spanish reader printed in Spain blatantly stereotype women, Indians and Asians.

darkskinned people—ignoring the African cultural heritage—*no* poor people, and *no* cultural authenticity.)

4. Do the non-English readers, math, science, and history textbooks reflect the infrastructure values of the child's own culture? Or are they reflective of the values of the dominant U.S. culture?

5. Does the material give as much space and respect to the third world perspective on events and people described as it does to the perspective of the dominant white group?

6. If the material is translated from English into the second language, is the quality of the translation equal to what publishers would demand in a reverse translation?

(Frequently books are translated by someone who knows, but is not at home with, the second language. This distorts idioms, leads to stilted writing, and to confused meaning.)

7. If the textbook uses two languages, does it imply that the second language is any less prestigious than English?

(Children should be made to feel that it is equally important for them to learn their first language well, as it is for them to learn English. No language or heritage should be considered superior to another.)

8. Does the textbook imply that Castilian Spanish is superior to Spanish used in other parts of Spain, in Puerto Rico, Mexico, or other Latin American countries? Does the textbook imply that the European Spanish heritage is *more* valuable than the African and Indian heritages which also are part of Latino cultures?

9. Are the textbooks too simplistic for the ages of the children using them and thus seen as an insulting putdown by the children?

(Many textbooks assume non-English speaking children have no understanding of basic shapes, grammar structure, etc.—assumptions which would not be made about English speaking children of the same age.)

10. Do the educators selecting the texts include some people for whom Spanish, Chinese, Vietnamese, etc. is their primary language? If that is not possible, can community parents be enlisted to aid in the selection process?

Bilingual textbooks, like English textbooks, ignore exciting stories about workers striking for better pay and working conditions. The story of the Chicana led pecan workers strike, in the 1930's, is one tale well suited for inclusion in basal readers or social studies textbooks.

Checklist For Career Education Textbooks

(credit note: The racism checklist was developed by the Council for a study of 100 randomly selected career education materials. The sexism checklist was developed by the Council based on a report by Women on Words and Images (WOWI) on 84 sets of career education materials. For availability of both these studies, see p. 104.)

Neither children's literature, social studies textbooks, TV, or movies prepare young people for the world of work. It is a generally ignored subject. Yet it is in the world of work that bias against white women, minority people, older people, and disabled people causes the most harm. Until we reach the day when statistics prove that job titles and average earnings are not directly related to one's sex, race, age, or disability, the United States will remain a land in which "freedom and justice for all" is more rhetoric than reality.

This places a heavy responsibility on educators involved in career education. To achieve an equitable society will require extensive affirmative action, not merely "equality of opportunity." White males are too far ahead in terms of "opportunity" for other groups to catch up without special efforts being made by government, business, and educators. And educators must find ways of showing particular concern for minority groups and females still hampered by bias, without diminishing their concern for the welfare of *all* pupils.

First, instructional materials must be carefully screened to see whether they offer positive role models for all students. (See section on "Real vs. Ideal," p. 29.) Second, classroom discussions must be initiated on bias in the workplace, and must include strategies for overcoming that bias. Third, career education materials must be kept from becoming a device used to "track" females and minorities to low-level jobs, aspirations, or educational goals. Tracking has served to reinforce the unequal distribution of income and status in our society and it must be brought to a halt. Fourth, the underlying assumption in instructional materials needs to be examined by a selection group which includes those people with a special sensitivity to employment discrimination in the market place. Fifth, since the content of career education texts and other materials has been documented as being both racist and sexist (and often anti-labor as well), checklists similar to those which follow should be given priority in all selection procedures.

RACISM CHECKLIST

VISUAL ANALYSIS
Overt Factors

What percentage of total number of workers shown are minority people? _____

Of this percentage, what is the percentage of males? _____ females ? _____

A = Virtually Always   U = Usually   OF = Often   O = Occasionally   N = Virtually Never

	A	U	OF	O	N
1. Are minority people *stereotyped* by skin color, facial features, hair styles, etc.?					

A = Virtually Always   U = Usually   OF = Often   O = Occasionally   N = Virtually Never

	A	U	OF	O	N
2. Are minority people isolated from white coworkers?					
3. Are minority people being supervised or taking directions?					
4. Are minority people supervising or training white workers?					
5. Are minority workers shown looking indecisive or confused?					
6. Are minority people shown as thinkers, planners, or highly skilled workers?					
7. Are minority workers shown as unskilled workers?					
8. Are minority people shown serving white people?					
9. Are white people shown serving minority people?					

Covert Factors

	A	U	OF	O	N
10. Where people are shown doing socially useful work, are minority people adequately and positively represented?					
11. Are minority people pictured against backgrounds that are culturally incongruous?					

CONTENT ANALYSIS (WRITTEN & ORAL)

Overt Factors:

	A	U	OF	O	N
1. Are relative advantages and disadvantages of each occupation discussed?					
2. Does the material state or imply that accents, physical characteristics, or other personal traits are disadvantages in an occupation?					
3. Does the material explain the worker's rights as well as responsibilities?					
4. Does the material explain the employer's responsibilities to the worker?					
5. Is testing used or suggested as the best way to determine one's ability to perform a job?					
6. Does the material use derogatory terms (e.g., "boy" instead of "man" when referring to an adult)?					
7. Does the material encourage optimal educational experiences rather than minimal/limited training?					
8. Do the materials encourage minority children to accept limited rights and limited roles?					

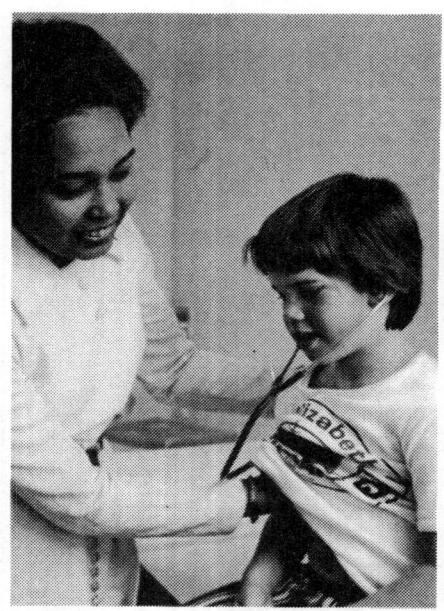

An unusually good career education text for very young children is *A Woman Is . . .*, by Aardvark Media in California. The caption for this photo reads, "A woman is a doctor who takes you by the hand, and walks with you and talks with you as only a doctor can."

This sexism study is discussed on the opposite page.

In the materials studied by the Council using the above checklist, underrepresentation of minorities was the norm. Stereotyping followed two patterns. In contrast to white workers who were given a variety of facial expressions and seemed to be taking their work quite seriously, Blacks invariably grinned, whether directing traffic, delivering mail, or even handling an important court case. Depictions of Blacks with Afro or corn row hair styles and adaptations of African clothing were rare, despite the popularity of these styles for the last decade. This results in a "proper Negro" with straightened hair stereotype. Non-Black minorities were generally difficult to identify, which may be interpreted as a subtle form of stereotyping.

Two other patterns occurred. One was tokenism, wherein the presence of one minority person was used to give evidence of inclusion. In addition, the sole minority person was commonly shown working alone. A second pattern was separatism, wherein minorities were shown working together, but with no whites present. When third world workers were shown serving whites, the work centered around food and hospitality services. When whites were shown serving third world people, it was in professional capacities such as social workers, public health services or police work.

In only three visual representations within the 100 materials examined were minority persons shown supervising or training white workers. In each case the supervisory position shown required a college degree and specialized training. This striking imbalance underscores the necessity for educators to counter the message communicated by the materials. There was also low representation of minority employees in all high-level positions.

In many instructional materials third world people were depicted as performing services in lily-white communities. This practice reinforces the theme that minority employment is designed to serve whites.

Testing was often recommended as the best way to see whether someone was suitable for a job. Since it is known that third world people do not do as well as whites on most tests (which are usually "normed" on whites) and since very few tests are actually related to work problems, this was perceived as discriminatory against minorities.

An incident of racism overlapping with sexism involved a third world woman being interviewed by a white male. The interviewer asked if she'd be willing to "tone down her dress" if she got the job. The gratuitous remark is culturally offensive, bright colors being traditionally a distinctive part of the dress of many minority groups. And, of course, the color of one's dress has no bearing whatsoever on the ability to perform a job.

The career education materials emphasize employment opportunities available to high school graduates. For jobs that require post-high school training, the two year community college was often suggested. Frank Riessman has written an editorial titled "The Vocationalization of Higher Education: Duping the Poor." An excerpt appears below.

> The danger in all this, of course, is that we will produce great numbers of new technicians, recruited largely from Black and other minority groups, who will have as their cut-off point a community-college education consisting mostly of training for fairly low-level jobs. But these technicians will be deprived of advanced knowledge related both to their jobs and to the world.

The occupational advantages discussed in the career education materials pertained to working conditions, entry level requirements, salaries, and fringe benefits. The most important characteristics about jobs—status, monetary rewards, and power—were seldom made clear. Many third world people point out that it is control over just these occupational advantages that is lacking in so many jobs held by minorities.

The materials examined were permeated by work-conditioning jargon supportive mainly of employer interests. Totally ignored is the proposition that workers take definitive action to protect their rights when they are treated unfairly. Only two books in the 100 materials reviewed dealt with racial job discrimination. Materials that fail to deal forthrightly with the issue lack educational validity. Third world students will be shortchanged and white students will be led to believe that minorities do not achieve in this society for reasons of their own making. This is another expression of the "blaming the victim" syndrome.

SEXISM CHECKLIST

	MALES		FEMALES	
	White	Minority	White	Minority
1. Number of workers who are				
2. Number of occupations with workers who are				
3. Number of high-status occupations with				
4. Number of workers in sex-traditional occupations				
5. Number of workers in non-traditional occupations				
6. In AV materials, number of narrators who sound				

7. When men and women are shown in non-traditional jobs, are they shown as tokens only?

8. Is sexist language and terminology used? (See pp. 35-7.)

9. Are females, but not males, advised on how to combine career and family?

10. Are females, but not males, warned to be careful of their grooming?

11. Are students told of bias in the work place and of how to combat it?

When Women on Words and Images conducted their survey they found that males were 62 per cent of all workers illustrated. Males narrated 37 sets of materials, females one set. Many more occupations were offered to male students than to female students. Most of the occupations offered were sex stereotyped. Sexist language was used much of the time. Women, but not men, were constantly warned about their appearance and were expected to have problems combining career and family.

On the whole, the findings in regard to sexism were even more dismal than were the findings in regard to racism.

BIAS IN U.S. HISTORY TEXTBOOKS

(credit note: The material in this section was taken from the report of a study of 14 widely used, secondary level history textbooks published during the 1970's. The report appeared under the title, Stereotypes, Distortions and Omissions in U.S. History Textbooks. *For availability of the entire study see p. 104.)*

Introduction

Before 1965, Chicanos, Puerto Ricans, and Asian Americans were nearly invisible in U.S. history textbooks. Women, AfroAmericans, and Native Americans were mentioned, though usually misrepresented through stereotyping, biased reporting, or omission of important information.

In today's textbooks, the groups previously invisible are granted a few more paragraphs than heretofore. Blacks and Native Americans receive more "sympathetic" treatment. A bit more attention is paid to other third world groups and to women as well.

However, heightened visibility does not necessarily assure an accurate depiction of reality. The Council survey has led to a number of observations about the way current textbooks present U.S. history. These observations fall into three general categories—"Perspective," "Methods of Inclusion," and "The Underlying Assumptions."

PERSPECTIVE

A basic problem with history textbooks is perspective, or point of view. The perspective dominating textbooks has always been white, upper class, and male. Generations of young people have been taught that the United States is a white country and that the prime architects of U.S. life and history are white males. This perspective continues in near ubiquity. *The American Experience, A Free People, The Pageant of American History, Man in America,* are all current texts with titles that do not reflect reality. There has always been more than one "American Experience"; people in the United States are "Free" to very different degrees; history, for many people, has not been a glorious "Pageant"; and "America" (an entire continent, not just the United States) is populated by more than "Man." Although new textbooks include some information that was previously omitted, too frequently the information is a porthole view *about* a people, but not *from the perspective of* the people described. In other instances, the information is set apart from the rest of the text which continues to reflect one viewpoint only.

SINGLE PERSPECTIVE

Numerous examples of this restricted perspective were found in each of the books surveyed. In the midst of several pages devoted to slavery and the life of "the slave," a statement like the following appears: "To live in the South was to live in daily fear of slave violence." Clearly, this statement speaks only for white people, as does, "Alone in the wilderness, the frontier family had to protect itself from wild animals and unfriendly Indians." Had the books represented other perspectives, these quotations might have read: "To live in the South was to live in the daily hope of a successful rebellion against slave-owners," or "While the people were trying to live, farm, and hunt peacefully in their homelands, they had to constantly be on guard against marauding and invading whites."

From book titles to chapter headings to text commentary, all of the textbooks depict U.S. history through the eyes of society's white majority—in particular, through the eyes of its more privileged members. Though these eyes are today more sensitive to the presence of others than they have previously been, they are nevertheless *particular,* not universal, eyes.

NARROW PERSPECTIVE

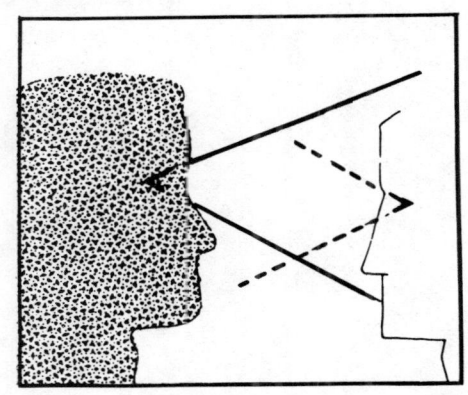

Because events are viewed through the eyes of the privileged, textbooks do not indicate that the lives and the aspirations of the average white citizens are linked to the lives and the interests of the third world people. This limitation is exemplified in a quotation like: "This 1896 ruling [*Plessy v. Ferguson*] by the Supreme Court was a serious blow to the efforts of black Americans to improve their lives."

Surely it was a "serious blow" to the efforts of Blacks, but by re-legalizing segregation, the decision had profoundly adverse effects on whites, too. By viewing *Plessy* as a Black problem the textbook subtly places the onus for overcoming obstacles onto the backs of Black people alone. A broader perspective would demonstrate that others, besides Black people, have an interest in, and responsibility for, ending segregation; others besides Native Americans, in ending the tragedy exemplified by the *Trail of Tears;* and others, not only Asian Americans, in protesting the internment of Japanese Americans during World War II; as does everyone have an interest in overcoming the oppression of women today. These issues affect *all* people in our society. A defeat for one group has repercussions on all, and results in prolonging the racist and sexist aspects of U.S. society.

EUROCENTRIC PERSPECTIVE

As with their older counterparts, there is a wide disparity between the way new textbooks report on the origins of U.S. minority cultures, compared to their treatment of the origins of the European colonists and immigrants. While Black reaction to white-imposed slavery is discussed, information about life in African countries is scant. Hence, students gain no sense of who African Americans were before they were brought to these shores nor any insights into the values, beliefs, cultures, and skills they brought with them. Similarly, Chicano life and culture prior to the U.S. annexation of their land is omitted. The heritages brought to the United States by Chinese, Japanese, and Filipino laborers remain obscure. And Puerto Rican culture, if discussed at all, is written off as being "Spanish."

The one exception, space-wise, is coverage of Native American cultures. Most textbook descriptions, however, are reserved for pre-Columbian societies and are too superficial and generalized to be of value. The continuity between pre-Columbian and present-day Native values and beliefs is ignored.

This one-sided, Eurocentric perspective emphasizes the importance of white roots and European backgrounds. It conveys the impression that third world people in the United States lack a cultural heritage, are definable *only* in terms of their relationship to white people, and are, therefore, inferior to whites.

METHODS OF INCLUSION

We observed that inclusion of people of color and women in textbooks takes three major forms: as "greats," as "contributors," and as "protestors."

INCLUSION AS "GREATS"

Basically, textbooks still recount history according to the "Great Man" approach, interpreting the past to be the activities and accomplishments of a relatively few statesmen, generals, inventors, and merchants—almost invariably white and male. In the newer texts, one finds that a few "Great Minorities" and "Great Women" have been added to the limited cast of characters.

While the inclusion of a few individual achievers from previously excluded groups is a positive improvement, a cautionary note must be sounded. Writing in *The Black Scholar* of March 1976, James Oliver Horton points out that the inclusion of such individuals "usually amounts to no more than spot appearances . . . in the dramatic production of the great American epic." Moreover, serious scrutiny of the communities from which these individuals came and from which they drew their strength "brings confrontation with the American myth. . . . The black experience, much like that of women, Indians and some other minorities, is distinctly 'un-American'" (that is, un-Euro-male-American). While the exceptional careers of a few individuals reinforce the Horatio Alger myth-pattern, the group experiences of the peoples, as a whole, illustrate the grave failures of the U.S. system.

Inevitably, by regarding a few individuals as the moving force in human history, and by underrepresenting the activities of working people, textbooks ignore the skills, concerns, and struggles of the average citizens who have played a primary role in creating and shaping events. Reading these books, female, third world, and poor students especially, must feel like powerless cogs unable to play any vital role.

WHO SELECTS THE "GREATS"?

Whether or not one adheres to the "Great Man" interpretation of history, there is no denying that textbooks create role models for young people when they select, for description, certain historical personages. It is interesting that older texts routinely preferred Booker T. Washington's "moderation" over W.E.B. DuBois' anti-establishment activities. They extolled the non-violent methods of Martin Luther King and ignored or deplored the angrier style of Malcolm X. John Brown was unfailingly described as a fanatic, while Abraham Lincoln's view—"If I could save the Union without freeing any slave I would do it"—was rarely criticized.

Newer texts still retain all the traditional white, male heros, but their wider cast of characters now includes a few alternative role models. But what if textbooks were to select heros through the eyes of different perspectives? Might they then praise Chicanos such as Joaquin Murieta and Juan Cortina who led resistance to the United States takeover of their lands after the war of conquest with Mexico? Might they admire Totanka Iotanka (Sitting Bull) and Tashunka Witko (Crazy Horse) who led their people in the defeat of Custer? Honor the actions of Sojourner Truth, Mother Jones, and Margaret Sanger? Describe Albizu Campos and Lolita Lebrón as Puerto Rican patriots and martyrs? Report approvingly of the Japanese Americans who resisted incarceration during World War II?

Such suppositions may seem very far fetched. But, in fact, they coincide with the perspectives of a significant number of third world people, feminists, and historians. Were textbooks to aim for a truly pluralistic scope, they would grant the legitimacy of resistance to white or male oppression and give it some page-space, along with the traditional heros and role models they now present to students.

William E.B. DuBois is generally ignored in textbooks because he was consistently critical of the "color-line" defining race relations in the U.S. Yet Blacks consider him an important leader and scholar.

INCLUSION AS "CONTRIBUTORS"

A frequent method of including third world people is by listing their "contributions": Native Americans gave "us" corn; African Americans gave "us" jazz; and Chinese Americans helped to build "our" railroads. The implication is that third world people, and their achievements, are valuable only insofar as they prove useful to "us." (In the case of Native Americans, their development of corn stands as a major scientific and agricultural achievement, important to their own societies and having global significance.) Overall, the achievements of women and third world people are minimized. They frequently are isolated in special sections and paragraphs, tangential to the central tale of the "Great White Men" who "forged this nation" and are presumably "us."

The "contributions" approach also overlooks the fact that the "contributors" have not benefited much from their contributions. For example, a new textbook will cite the military service of tens of thousands of Blacks during World War I, but will ignore discrimination in the armed forces and the segregation and racism to which Black veterans returned. Or when discussing the bounty of the U.S. corn belt, texts never note that Native Americans fail to share in the national wealth made possible by their development of corn and their "contribution" of the land upon which it is grown.

This excellent book, published by Design Enterprises of San Francisco, offers supplementary information missing from most history texts.

Textbooks would be more informative if they explained that the unpaid, underpaid, and/or unheralded work of third world people and women, plus the land expropriated from Native Americans, Chicanos and Puerto Ricans, were usually *coerced contributions* which have primarily benefited the white community. Textbooks should also convey to students that *all* of the people who make up the U.S. population share claim to the benefits which have evolved out of the labor and skill of many groups. Not to do so is to reinforce the idea that white people are "us"—and third world people are "other." This fosters alienation and resentment in third world students, and it also fosters an unrealistic sense of superiority in white students.

INCLUSION AS PROTESTORS

A good deal of the expanded treatment of third world people and women in the newer texts focuses on the liberation movements of the 1960's and 1970's. Unfortunately for students, these movements are not placed in any sort of historical context that might show them as part of a long continuum of social and political protest. Some books imply by omission, and others state outright, that political protest and self-liberation efforts are but recent developments. In this way, textbooks doom new generations to act unknowingly, instead of building on a careful study of the thoughts and actions, the successes and mistakes of those who struggled in the past. Denied knowledge of these details of their history, young people are forced today to reinvent the wheel.

Today's textbooks also fail to connect the present struggles of third world people in the United States with liberation movements around the globe, and are vague as to which groups, or what circumstances, stand in opposition to such efforts.

INCLUSION OF CHOSEN PROTESTORS

While presenting a paucity of information on current liberation struggles, textbooks emphasize intra- and inter-group *divisions,* and tend to ignore intra- and inter-group *unity.* Textbooks also avoid any serious consideration of the variety of goals and methods which characterize liberation movements. For instance, some feminists view the opportunity to become highly paid, decision-making executives as a liberating goal, yet others feel that the revamping of the basic economic and patriarchal structure must be the primary focus. Similar differences in aims exist within all third world groups. However, the textbooks seriously discuss only those organizations and individuals who want a larger "piece of the pie," that is, reform within the present social and economic system. They scarcely recognize those groups who want truly basic change, be it social, political, or economic.

Although the United States was born in violent revolution, a new text states: "Americans throughout our history have believed that all men must obey the law if democracy is to continue . . . No man can put himself above the law. . . . Most Americans still believe freedom is based on government by law." Textbooks imply that only *legal* protest is legitimate, rather than indicating that progress has been achieved through active and passive resistance, violent and non-violent tactics, legal and extra-legal methods. On the whole, textbooks present neither the limitations of electoral and legal reforms, nor the viability (and often necessity) of other options.

THE UNDERLYING ASSUMPTIONS

The photographer of this man (who is angry about slum conditions in the Puerto Rican barrio in New York City) is Michael Abramson. He is quoted, in *The Eye of Conscience: photographers and social change* by Milton Meltzer and Bernard Cole, as saying, "It is time for photographers to stop photographing the victims of America and begin to record the struggle of those who fight against their victimization." Bravo! Textbooks should also record such struggles!

Implicit in all of the textbooks surveyed is the assumption that U.S. society is a true democracy, by virtue of its electoral system in which citizens can vote for the leader of their choice. Democracy is never defined as people controlling the institutions which daily affect them and their families, workplaces, schools, courts, and so on. Furthermore, it is assumed that a democratic government like ours is the best of all possible governments. Perhaps it really *is* best, but the textbooks describe "communist" and "socialist" nations by their economic systems, while rarely describing U.S. society in terms of its capitalist economic system. This muddies comparisons of both economies and governments. The distortion which results is serious, for by calling both our government and economic system "democratic," the textbooks deny the realities of capitalism and all that goes with it—classes, conflicting class interests, and the ongoing struggle between those few who control wealth and those many who are trying to share the wealth.

Stemming from this refusal to recognize the conflict of class interests is the refusal to link sexism and racism to economic exploitation. While the newer books have broadened previous descriptions of poverty and economic hardship and are now more "sympathetic" towards third world people and women, the resulting picture has no depth of composition. No group, no institution, no system seems to bear responsibility for these conditions. There are victims, but no victimizers; exploited, but no exploiters. Those who benefit from the system, and their profit motivations, are left invisible.

The situation of farmworkers may be described as deplorable, but the combination of agribusiness, government officials, and Teamster Union officials who fought against decent working and living conditions for farmworkers for years is neither stated, described, nor condemned. Also pictured as deplorable are urban ghettos. Yet no connection is made to an unfair economic system, redlining banks, or other institutions which perpetuate ghettos for profit. Texts may say that women are paid lower wages, but no mention is made of who profits from the pay differentials. Discrimination, racism, and sexism are never analyzed as *structures* which profit some people at the expense of others.

BLAMING THE VICTIM

Students might well conclude that women and third world people are unsuccessful by nature, heredity, or inclination. The presentations in the texts would not dissuade, but instead actually encourage such assumptions, for even the new texts tend to "blame the victims" for their own oppressed circumstances. Native Americans were dispossessed of their land because they "did not understand the concept of private land ownership"; Asian workers received low wages because they were "willing to work for very little"; Blacks could not find good urban jobs because they were "unskilled and uneducated"; Chicanos face problems because they are "not fluent in English"; Filipinos and Puerto Ricans were colonized because they were "not ready for self-government"; and women "lack sufficient physical strength" and are "too frequently pregnant" to be an important part of the workforce.

Texts may imply that individual bigots, or groups of ignorant and prejudiced people, are to blame for some unfortunate situations, while ignoring a society that manipulates and encourages working class divisions. Or texts may imply that poverty is a temporary condition, which people will leave behind as they increase their education and skills. Because the economic system is not held accountable, students are led to believe that education and greater tolerance will eliminate societal flaws, and that 300 years of institutional racism against third world people, and many more years of patriarchal repression against women, will gradually wither away.

SUMMARY

To the extent that discrimination, racism, and sexism are dealt with in textbooks, they are treated as aberrations, as isolated mistakes of the past. Since oppression is rarely examined from the perspective of its victims, these brief inclusions appear as footnotes to a grander, happier story. Yet even those isolated "mistakes" are treated in a simplistic, casual manner which downplays their significance. The internment of 110,000 Japanese in concentration camps was not an isolated "mistake" when seen in the light of the systematic mistreatment of, and hostility towards, Japanese and other Asians working and living in this country. The *Trails of Tears* of the Cherokee, Choctaw, Chickasaw, Seminole, and Creek nations were not aberrations, but elements of systematic and continuous national policy that led to the extermination of millions. The adoption of a pro-slavery constitution was not a "temporary" compromise; rather it was a logical result of 150 years of enslaving African people as free labor to profit white people. The effects of that compromise were not "temporary," but still exist today. Racism, sexism, and economic exploitation are not occasional aberrations of the U.S. system, but deeply ingrained mechanisms of the national social and economic structure. By isolating specific events from the overall context of a people's historical experiences, their histories are fragmented and downplayed. By failing to compare the experiences of different peoples (e.g., reservations for Native Americans, concentration camps for Japanese), the evolution of recurrent, basic themes is lost.

This bibliography, prepared by women in Cambridge, Mass., is useful for finding books to fill the missing textbook pages on women's history.

The role of economic gain for the dominant group is a solid pillar in the development and play of U.S. history, from the days of exploration and settlement to the separation from Britain, from the opening of the interior and the building of railroads to the concentration of capital and the industrial and technological revolutions. In a sense, the faulty and idealistic transmission of U.S. history has contributed to keeping working women and men ignorant of the forces which limit their options and frustrate their goals. An honest, pluralistic presentation of the history of all peoples in these United States would go some distance to help students achieve greater control in directing their own—and their country's—future.

Examples of History Textbook Bias

PERSPECTIVE—All textbooks reflect—consciously or unconsciously—the interpretations of their authors. Authors usually present information from the experiences and viewpoints of certain groups and ignore the experiences and viewpoints of other groups. While no book can be totally "objective," it is especially important for history textbooks to view an event from the varying perspectives of the groups involved; otherwise students will achieve only a partial understanding of the event itself.

So they drew up a plan of government called the Mayflower Compact, which all of the men signed. According to the Mayflower Compact, all the people would share in setting up a government for the new Colony.
America: Its People and Values, p. 73

This text doesn't seem to view the women on the Mayflower as *people*, so it doesn't mention that women were not allowed to sign the Compact or set up the government.

To live in the South was to live in daily fear of slave violence.
The Pageant of American History, p. 211

Certainly not the perspective of the slave!

MYTH—A myth is an ill-founded belief that is perpetuated in the face of contrary facts. Textbooks frequently perpetuate myths which support the status quo.

Americans throughout our history have believed that all *men must obey the law if democracy is to continue. If a law is wrong, the constitution provides ways of changing the law. No man need break it. No man can put himself above the law.*
American History for Today, p. 193

The United States itself was born in violent revolution, and throughout our history, people have agitated and struggled against injustice. Abolitionism, women's suffrage, civil rights, union organizing, and anti-war activities are among the struggles which have utilized extra-legal tactics of boycotts, passive resistance, civil disobedience, and breaking of law. Changes in the law to correct injustice have often resulted *because* of extra-legal types of agitation.

STEREOTYPE—An untruth or oversimplification about the traits and behaviors common to an entire people is a stereotype. The stereotype is applied to each member of the group, without regard to that person's individual character. Authors, like other people, often believe stereotypes common within their own culture. Such stereotypes then distort what they report about particular groups of people.

[Ku Klux Klan] members dressed in grotesque robes and hoods. These costumes were supposed to frighten the superstitious "darkies." They also made the white wearers feel self-important, just as the ritual paint and feathers did that were worn by Indian braves.
The Impact of Our Past, p. 403

This text puts "darkies" in quotes, but leaves "superstitious" without quotation marks. This suggests that Black people were (are) superstitious. It also perpetuates the stereotype of Native American males wearing paint and feathers, a cultural practice of a few Native nations that white society has applied as a stereotype to all "Indians." Finally, the quote applies the stereotyped term *braves* to Native American men.

In California, descendants of Japanese immigrants have become very successful farmers. A number of Japanese-Americans are now outstanding photographers, architects and professors in American universities.
America: Its People and Values, p. 56

Though the comparative situation of Japanese Americans has improved, the "successful minority" stereotype obscures problems they still face. Middle-class Japanese Americans are often denied advancement opportunities. While the median income for Japanese American families is higher than the national average, in over 50 per cent of most families both wife and husband work, as compared to 39 per cent in other U.S. families. In Nihonmanchi (the Japanese equivalent to Chinatown), elderly Issei and Nisei are often unable to obtain necessary social services or medical care. "Urban renewal" has destroyed large sections of many such communities, which are the cultural and social centers of the Japanese American population. The "fat Jap" remark of Spiro Agnew and the "little Jap" remark made during the U.S. Senate Watergate hearings are indicative of the prejudice Japanese Americans still confront.

CHARACTERIZATION—Many words and descriptions are commonly used, intentionally or unintentionally, to create negative images of groups of people. The repeated use of such characterization reinforces stereotypes. Examples are: *savage, lazy, massacre, primitive, warlike, squaw, crafty, inscrutable, greasy, gossipy, scatterbrained.*

To bring their cause to America's attention, women paraded in the streets. They pestered Congressmen. They formed groups and gave speeches.
American History for Today, pp. 366-368

The characterization of women "pestering" is similar to those of women "bickering" or "gossiping." By contrast, men would be said to have "lobbied" Congress.

In San Francisco the historically compliant Chinese aggressively resisted attempts to bus their children to schools outside of Chinatown.
The American Experience, p. 832

Labeling Chinese as compliant is to perpetuate the stereotype of a submissive, passive people. This characterization ignores the long history of struggle by Chinese working people.

DISTORTION—Textbooks can twist the meaning of history by slanting their presentation of facts, resulting in a distorted view of history. Distortion can also occur by the omission of information that would alter the viewpoint being presented.

Today . . . Puerto Ricans enjoy a per capita income higher than that of any other Latin-American country with the single exception of oil-rich Venezuela.
Rise of the American Nation, p. 832

Puerto Rico has been controlled by the United States since 1898, so its per capita income should also be compared with U.S. per capita income—a comparison in which Puerto Rico would rank well below any U.S. state.

Three and a half million blacks became free men. Many southerners did not know how to live without slaves. Many former slaves did not know how to live without their former masters. The law had made them free but had left them helpless.
The Pageant of American History, p. 281

This distorts the meaning of "free men" (not to mention the fact that half of them were free women). Perhaps white Southerners did not like to live without slaves (the author forgets that the slaves were also Southerners), but the skilled Black farmworkers and artisans knew full well how to live without their former masters, *provided* they were given some way in which to earn a living. Calling them "helpless" is a gross distortion, covering up the irresponsibility of the federal government in not giving the freed people sufficient aid.

Japanese-Americans living on the Pacific Coast were especially hard hit. They were victims of hysteria brought on by the war.
In Search of America, p. 79-D

It was the long-practiced racism against Japanese on the West Coast—not war-time "hysteria" or "national security"—that led to the internment of over 110,000 Japanese living in the United States. In Hawaii, a more militarily vulnerable area with a far larger proportion of Japanese, no internment took place.

In addition to that distortion there is a basic omission. The text neglects to point out that the United States was also at war with Germany and Italy, but did not intern "white" German Americans and Italian Americans.

OMISSION—One way of distorting history and maintaining myths is to omit certain information and viewpoints which do not support the author's views. Such omissions seriously distort a reader's understanding of events.

Members of the Sons of Liberty, an organization formed soon after passage of the Stamp Act, expressed their anti-British attitudes by encouraging non-importation, tarring and feathering loyalists and British tax agents, destroying property, and threatening British officials with bodily harm.
The American Experience, p. 37

Prior to the Revolution, the boycotting of English imports was organized primarily by women. This was an important method of economic warfare. Women organized and participated in demonstrations against the British and against colonists cooperating with the British. Much of this was done through the "Daughters of Liberty." It is thought by some historians that the famed Committees of Correspondence were actually initiated by Mercy Otis Warren—a well-known propagandist, author, and historian—but were credited to her husband, as only a male signature would be taken seriously. Women were also key to the success of the Revolution, though no texts include that information.

Included among those who served [in WW I] were tens of thousands of black Americans. Most served in laboring jobs, but a number of individuals and units won fame in battle against the Germans. American Negroes fought especially well as parts of larger French units.
American History for Today, p. 398

This omits information on the paradox of segregated Black troops fighting "to make the world safe for democracy," and the racism they faced when they returned to the United States. These were critical realities to the Blacks, and their omission distorts the understanding that students receive of U.S. society.

ETHNOCENTRISM—People often feel that their own group's values, culture, and standards are superior to all others. They develop a perspective which judges other people's culture and customs as different from, and therefore inferior to, their own. Authors, historians, and students can try to develop an understanding of other viewpoints, values, and customs and recognize that all have legitimacy on their own terms. Judging other cultures by the standards of one's own culture is ethnocentric.

The Spaniards had established a capital city at Monterey, in 1769. And, led by a remarkable Franciscan leader, Junipero Serra, these Spaniards began building a series of missions. . . . the work of the missions was successful. Many of the California Indians were converted to the Roman Catholic religion. Except for these Spanish mission settlements, and a few outposts, most of California was unsettled land.
America: Its People and Values, p. 408

This implies that converting Native Americans to Christianity is a positive act, all the while ignoring the functional and legitimate religious practices and beliefs of Native people. The ethnocentric presumption is that Christianity was superior to Native American religions. The quote also ignores the fact that Native Americans were living throughout the area of California, so it was not, at least in their eyes, an "unsettled land."

In 1917, the Puerto Ricans were granted citizenship. As American citizens, Puerto Ricans could migrate freely from Puerto Rico to the mainland of the United States and back again whenever they chose to do so.
The Pageant of American History, p. 417

The tone implies that U.S. citizenship is desirable to all people. It is not surprising, with that ethnocentric attitude, that the following information was omitted:

Citizenship was imposed by an act of the U.S. Congress. Puerto Rico's elected resident commissioner in Washington pleaded that a referendum be held to determine the people's wishes on the issue, but he was ignored. In 1913 the only Puerto Rican-elected legislature had *unanimously* refused U.S. citizenship, stating: "We firmly and loyally oppose our being declared, against our express will or without our express consent, citizens of any other than our own beloved country. . . ."

EUROCENTRISM—In presenting information from the perspective of EuroAmericans on this continent, authors often ignore the experiences, motivations, aspirations, and views of non-EuroAmericans. To interpret the experiences and actions both of EuroAmericans and of people of color only from the perspective of EuroAmericans and not give similar space and legitimacy to the other perspectives, is Eurocentric.

In reality, Columbus "rediscovered" the New World. Other Europeans had explored there many years before. . . . Other Europeans may also have "discovered" the New World before Columbus. . . . However, after Columbus' voyage the Americas stayed discovered.
Rise of the American Nation, p. 10

As the settlers pushed inland, they found the Indians living in areas the settlers wanted. The Indians did not understand the settlers' idea of land ownership. They thought the land belongs to all people who needed it.
America: Its People and Values, p. 564

To state—as the first quote does—that Europeans *discovered* a hemisphere occupied by millions of people is totally Eurocentric. Native Americans were well aware that the hemisphere existed (and evidence also suggests that Africans and Chinese had travelled to the Americas before Europeans). The second quote assumes that private ownership of land is more natural or legitimate than communal use. It places responsibility on Native Americans for not understanding the European concept of land ownership. Not only was the cultural relationship of Native Americans to the land legitimate, but since it was *their* land in the first place, it was the European settlers who failed to understand the Native American viewpoint.

SEXISM—Sexism is any attitude, action, or institutional practice which subordinates a person or group because of their sex. Since most authors, editors, and historians are, and have been, male, and all have been reared in a patriarchal society, they reflect the perspective that male activity is most important and that the viewpoints and actions of females are of little consequence. U.S. institutions have always been controlled by males, and have been run for the advantage of males.

There are times in the lives of men and of nations when the world seems to stand still. April, 1865, was such a time. After years of work and hardships, the American people were at peace. Everywhere, men tried to understand the meaning of what had happened. (Emphasis added)
  America: Its People and Values, p. 476

By use of the term "men," the quote ignores the fact that women were over half the population.

In the 1830's and 1840's some workers began to join trade unions. These were associations which united workingmen to improve their wages and working conditions. The unions led strikes to force employers to grant their demands. (Emphasis added)
  The Impact of Our Past, p. 320

This ignores the fact that women were workers, active in union organizing and strikes during that period. Both quotes demonstrate more than the use of sexist language. They demonstrate the invisibility of women in textbooks.

A fifth type of reform was aimed at raising the moral tone of all society by getting people to change habits that the reformers thought were bad. The move for temperance (prohibition or strict control over the drinking of liquor) was one of these.
  The Impact of Our Past, p. 321

The temperance movement aimed at much more than "raising the moral tone." Women and children suffered, without legal recourse, when their husbands and fathers drank. Women could not leave or divorce their husbands, or legally protect themselves from physical abuse. The law made women responsible for their husbands' debts, and the law did not force men to support their families. Many temperance leaders later became active in the women's rights movement. Yet textbooks traditionally belittle women for temperance activities.

RACISM—Racism is any attitude, action, or institutional practice which functions to subordinate a person or group because of their color. In the United States, the institutions which compose our society (education, business, unions, banks, government, etc.) are controlled by whites. Thus, because white society exercises institutional power to oppress third world people, we refer to white racism when we use the term racism. The control of institutional power distinguishes racism from individual prejudice. All people in our society can hold prejudiced attitudes and beliefs.

Under the Indian Reorganization Act [1934], tribal governments were formed. Indian leaders gained confidence as they gained experience.
  Man In America, p. 546

[The Filipinos] were weak and defenseless. They had no experience in governing themselves. . . . President McKinley and Congress finally accepted responsibility for governing the islands of the Philippines. . . . The United States tried to help the Filipinos to develop their land into a democratic nation. Step by step, the Filipinos learned to govern themselves.
  America: Its People and Values, p. 683

Each of these quotes suggests that people of color are unable to govern themselves without the paternalistic guidance of the United States. Such implications perpetuate the racism of "manifest destiny" and the "white man's burden." No textbook presents similar assumptions when discussing the settlement of Europeans in the Americas and the development of their governmental practices.

The Prentice Hall book on the right is a good introduction to the subject of institutional racism.

AFRICAN AMERICAN CHECKLIST

There are 21 criteria to be scored. The highest possible rating is +42. The lowest is –42. This text scores _____.

	Incorrect information (-2)	No Information (-1)	Omits This Period (0)	Limited Information (+1)	Full Information (+2)
1. African, as well as European, culture forms an integral part of the U.S. heritage.					
2. Africans were in the Americas prior to 1619.					
3. The North American slave trade created enormous profits, became the most brutal system of slavery known, and disrupted African civilization.					
4. The significance of the Revolution, to Blacks, goes beyond participation in combat.					
5. The Constitution was a pro-slavery document and remained so for 78 years.					
6. Slavery was inherently cruel and inhuman.					
7. Rebellion and slavery went hand in hand.					
8. While there were differences in the institution between North and South, slavery was never a regional issue.					
9. Blacks initiated anti-slavery activity and were central to the abolition leadership.					
10. The life of the free African American was often only a slight improvement over the life of a slave.					
11. Blacks who participated in the take over of the West were also oppressed by white society.					
12. The lack of land redistribution was the fundamental failure of Reconstruction.					
13. When freedpeople had land, they displayed incentive and skill, establishing productive lives.					
14. Sharecropping resulted in the economic re-enslavement of Black people.					
15. The Reconstruction governments were more progressive and democratic than later southern governments.					
16. Post-Reconstruction brought a rigidly segregated society, with full Federal support.					
17. The racism of organized labor has harmed Black people and disrupted the potential for working-class unity.					
18. Woodrow Wilson's "progressive" policies were meant "for whites only."					
19. Discrimination faced by European immigrants was different from the racism faced by Blacks.					
20. Institutional racism, not merely individual prejudice, causes and perpetuates racial inequality.					
21. The myth of "progress" obscures the existing reality of the majority of Black people.					
Total					
Textbook Final Score					

ASIAN AMERICAN CHECKLIST

CHINESE AMERICAN

There are 13 criteria to be scored. The highest possible rating is +26.
The lowest is −26. This text scores _____.

	Incorrect information −2	No Information −1	Omits This Period 0	Limited Information +1	Full Information +2
1. Multiple reasons caused the Chinese to come to the United States.					
2. Anti-Chinese bias existed in the United States prior to the time Chinese arrived.					
3. The Chinese experienced both suffering and exploitation in building the railroad.					
4. Chinese worked at many occupations and were instrumental in developing some industries.					
5. Racism systematically excluded Chinese from entering into, or remaining in, some fields of work.					
6. Chinese workers organized to resist exploitation.					
7. Racism was utilized to divide Chinese from other workers.					
8. The widespread violence against Chinese was backed by institutional support.					
9. There were numerous national, state and local anti-Chinese laws.					
10. The 1882 Chinese Exclusion Act had extensive ramifications.					
11. Sixty years of exclusion had devastating social consequences to Chinese in the United States.					
12. Chinatowns in the United States suffer the problems common to other urban ghettos.					
13. Chinese have a long history of struggle against oppression.					
Total					
Textbook Final Score					

JAPANESE AMERICAN

There are 11 criteria to be scored. The highest possible rating is +22.
The lowest is −22. This text scores _____.

	Incorrect information −2	No Information −1	Omits This Period 0	Limited Information +1	Full Information +2
1. United States sugar interests in Hawaii recruited and exploited Japanese laborers.					
2. Japanese undertook a variety of occupations in the United States.					
3. There was extensive legal, social, and economic persecution of Japanese in this country.					
4. Theodore Roosevelt manifested anti-Japanese sentiments and actions.					
5. The United States broke the Gentlemen's Agreement, in 1924, by excluding Japanese.					

	Incorrect information	No Information	Omits This Period	Limited Information	Full Information
	-2	-1	0	+1	+2
6. Curtailment of immigration had harmful social consequences upon Japanese in the United States.					
7. Placing Japanese in concentration camps during World War II was an action consistent with the long history of U.S. racism.					
8. Alien and native born Japanese, as well as some Japanese from outside the United States, were interned.					
9. Japanese Americans received less than 10 cents on the dollar as compensation for their property losses.					
10. Japanese Americans have not forgiven or forgotten the concentration camps.					
11. Describing Japanese Americans as a "successful minority" is a stereotype.					
Total					
Textbook Final Score					

FILIPINO AMERICAN

There are 9 criteria to be scored. The highest possible rating is +18.
The lowest is -18. The text scores _____.

1. Filipinos had struggled against Spanish rule, and were almost victorious before the United States arrived.					
2. The United States may have instigated a battle with Filipino forces to influence the U.S. Senate vote on the Treaty of Paris.					
3. The United States spent hundreds of millions of dollars and three years to brutally suppress the Filipino independence effort.					
4. The United States exploited the Philippines in a classic colonial fashion.					
5. Filipinos were recruited to the United States as low-paid labor when other Asians were excluded.					
6. Filipinos in the United States were subjected to violence, institutional racism and immigration restrictions.					
7. Filipino workers have a long history of struggling for their rights.					
8. Filipinos in the United States today still suffer from racism and exploitation.					
9. On July 4, 1946 the Philippines became a neo-colony of the United States.					
Total					
Textbook Final Score					

CHICANO CHECKLIST

There are 18 criteria to be scored. The highest possible rating is +36.
The lowest is −36. This text scores ―――――――.

	Incorrect information −2	No Information −1	Omits This Period 0	Limited Information +1	Full Information +2
1. The Native peoples of central and southern Mexico had attained high levels of civilization before the arrival of Spaniards.					
2. Many cities in the southwest United States were originally settled by La Raza.					
3. U.S. citizens living in Texas were foreign guests of Mexico.					
4. The U.S. takeover of Texas was a conspiracy planned by pro-slavery forces.					
5. Mexican forces were defenders, not invaders, of Texas.					
6. Texas and California had large non-Anglo populations.					
7. The war against Mexico was not caused by cultural conflicts, but by U.S. expansionism.					
8. The war against Mexico was considered unjust by many U.S. citizens of that time.					
9. The United States won almost a third of its present territory through the Mexican-American war.					
10. The Treaty of Guadalupe Hidalgo was not honored by the United States.					
11. For many years after the end of the war, Chicanos resisted the U.S. takeover of their country.					
12. The development of the Southwest was not achieved solely by Anglos.					
13. The recruitment and deportation of Mexican workers have reflected the need of U.S. business.					
14. Racism and violence against Chicanos was widespread through World War II.					
15. Chicanos have an ongoing history of resistance to oppression.					
16. The struggle of the United Farm Workers' Union has met violent resistance by a combination of powerful forces.					
17. Most Chicanos are urban dwellers and non-farm workers.					
18. Chicano poverty is the result of past and present racism.					
Total					
Textbook Final Score					

NATIVE AMERICAN CHECKLIST

There are 26 criteria to be scored. The highest possible rating is +52.
The lowest is −52. The text scores _____.

	Incorrect information −2	No Information −1	Omits This Period 0	Limited Information +1	Full Information +2
1. Native Americans are the original inhabitants of North America.					
2. Pre-Columbian Native American societies reflected great diversity and complexity.					
3. The myth of "discovery" is blatantly Eurocentric.					
4. At least ten to twelve million native peoples may have lived in what later became the United States.					
5. "Advanced culture" is an ethnocentric concept and does not explain or justify European conquest.					
6. War and violence were not characteristic of Indian nations.					
7. Native American technology and knowledge were achievements in their own right.					
8. Missionary activities were an integral part of European conquest.					
9. Native nations made alliances with European nations for their own strategic purposes.					
10. Conflicting European and colonial economic interests in Native lands helped trigger the U.S. revolution.					
11. Native nations fought the invaders to maintain their communities and lands.					
12. Land has a special significance to Native Americans and has been the central issue of conflict with the United States.					
13. It is Eurocentric to categorize Native Peoples as either "friendly" or "unfriendly."					
14. United States policies toward Native Americans reflect many political and economic factors within U.S. society.					
15. Textbook terminology is Eurocentric, ignoring Native American presence and perspectives.					
16. Legally binding treaties are central to the relations between Indian nations and the United States.					
17. The 1881 Dawes Act resulted in the loss of three-quarters of the remaining land of Native Americans.					
18. The Citizenship Act of 1924 was not a benevolent action.					
19. The Reorganization Act of 1934 heightened Native American alienation and powerlessness.					
20. The termination policy of the 1950's resulted in the loss of more land and the abrogation of treaties.					
21. The BIA is a corrupt and inefficient bureaucracy controlling the affairs of one million people.					
22. Oppressive conditions led to a proportionately lower population increase for Native Americans.					
23. Reservations represent a paradox for Native Americans.					

	Incorrect information	No Information	Omits This Period	Limited Information	Full Information
	-2	-1	0	+1	+2
24. Treaty rights, sovereignty, self-determination and the return of land are the major goals of Native Peoples.					
25. The struggle to maintain land continues today.					
26. There is a relationship between the past experiences and the present reality of Native Americans.					
Total					
Textbook Final Score					

PUERTO RICAN CHECKLIST

There are 19 criteria to be scored. The highest possible rating is +38. The lowest is −38. This text scores _____.

	Incorrect information	No Information	Omits This Period	Limited Information	Full Information
	-2	-1	0	+1	+2
1. The histories of Taino and African peoples are important in understanding Puerto Rican history.					
2. Puerto Ricans have a long history of striving for independence.					
3. The United States declared war on Spain in order to establish its own hegemony in this hemisphere.					
4. Puerto Ricans had mixed reactions to the United States take-over of their country.					
5. Puerto Rico had greater autonomy under Spanish rule than it has today under the United States.					
6. The Foraker Act formalized U.S. domination of Puerto Rico.					
7. U.S. citizenship was imposed on Puerto Ricans despite their protests.					
8. The United States established an educational system designed to "Americanize" Puerto Rico.					
9. Commonwealth status retained all significant aspects of U.S. control of Puerto Rico.					
10. Despite severe repression, the struggle for Puerto Rican independence continues.					
11. Operation Bootstrap led to the industrialization of Puerto Rico for the benefit of U.S. capital.					
12. Operation Bootstrap has not changed Puerto Rico's relative economic position vis-á-vis the United States.					
13. Puerto Rican women face a double oppression.					
14. Extensive migration was caused by U.S. exploitation of the country.					
15. Puerto Rican migrants in the United States face national and racial oppression not experienced by white immigrants.					
16. Puerto Rican life in the United States is characterized by circular migration to the homeland.					
17. Institutional racism results in the miseducation of Puerto Rican students in the United States.					
18. Puerto Rican culture is a synthesis of Taino, African, and Spanish cultures.					
19. Migrant farm workers from Puerto Rico are exploited by U.S. agribusiness.					
Total					
Textbook Final Score					

WOMEN'S CHECKLIST

There are 35 criteria to be scored. The highest possible rating is +70.
The lowest is −70. This text scores _____.

	Incorrect information −2	No Information −1	Omits This Period 0	Limited Information +1	Full Information +2
1. The original American women, Native Americans, wielded considerable power within their own societies.					
2. Native women were not the overworked "drudges" described by many white observers.					
3. Pocahontas and Sacajawea were not typical of Native American women.					
4. The early European settlers included many hardworking women.					
5. Textbook use of the English language obscures women's lack of legal and human rights, in colonial days and in the present.					
6. Ann Hutchinson and other women challenged the male monopoly of religious leadership.					
7. Women were imported to the colonies by London investors because their work and presence were profitable to business.					
8. As indentured servants imported as cheap labor by wealthier colonists, women were oppressed more than men servants.					
9. Most non-enslaved women enjoyed a greater degree of economic and social freedom than did European women of that time.					
10. Women played a key role in the Revolution as organizers, fund raisers, food growers and nurses.					
11. After the Revolution, women's options and freedoms were curtailed.					
12. Differences also sharpened between the lives of ordinary, and of rich, women.					
13. From the earliest industrial era, women's labor was especially exploited.					
14. Women's right to education, like all extensions of human rights, was achieved through a determined struggle.					
15. Women reformers accomplished major changes in U.S. society, affecting the quality of life.					
16. Many advocates of abolition—a cause in which women activists predominated—were also advocates of women's rights.					
17. The 1848 Seneca Falls Convention signified the historic start of the suffrage movement.					
18. Because women lacked legal rights, alcoholism posed a greater threat to them than it did to men.					
19. Enslaved Black women struggled against sexual, as well as racial, oppression.					
20. Black women also resisted oppressive laws.					
21. Women of all colors played a significant role in the Civil War.					
22. Women were essential to the "settlement" of the West.					

	Incorrect information -2	No Information -1	Omits This Period 0	Limited Information +1	Full Information +2
23. Wyoming and other western states granted women rights when it benefited the states to do so, not for moral reasons.					
24. Many Black women were active social reformers in the late 1800's and early 1900's.					
25. Women social reformers had significant impact upon aspects of urban life.					
26. In the early 1900's women workers were especially exploited. Some organized, despite lack of union interest in their conditions.					
27. The 1920 victory for women's suffrage represented years of effort and sacrifice.					
28. Suffrage did not succeed in making women's condition equal to men's.					
29. The availability of birth control information was, perhaps, more important to women than suffrage.					
30. The 1920's "flapper" era did not significantly liberate women.					
31. White ethnic immigrants had greater chances for upward mobility than did Black women and men.					
32. The great labor struggles of the 1930's actively involved women of all colors.					
33. Women's labor has often been recruited, abused and discarded by business interests, especially during labor shortages.					
34. Poor third world women face triple oppression today—race, sex, class.					
35. Institutional change, not mere passage of the Equal Rights Amendment, is necessary to improve the status of U.S. women.					
Total					
Textbook Final Score					

AVAILABLE MATERIALS

From Council on Interracial Books for Children, 1841 Broadway, New York, N.Y. 10023

CATALOG listing filmstrips, books, flyers, curriculums, etc.	Free
HUMAN AND ANTI-HUMAN VALUES IN CHILDREN'S BOOKS	$7.95
STEREOTYPES, DISTORTIONS and OMISSIONS in U.S. HISTORY TEXTBOOKS	$7.95
TEN QUICK WAYS to Identify Sexism and Racism in Children's Books	$1.50 for 10
DEFINITIONS OF RACISM	$1.50 for 10
RACISM IN THE ENGLISH LANGUAGE	$2.00
UNLEARNING "INDIAN" STEREOTYPES	$3.50
RACISM IN CAREER EDUCATION MATERIALS	$2.50
CHRONICLES OF AMERICAN INDIAN PROTEST	$5.95
BULLETIN Special Issues	
Asian Americans in Children's Books	$3.00
Puerto Ricans in Children's Books	$3.00
Chicanos in Children's Books	$3.00
Handicapism in Children's Books	$3.00
American Sign Language and Deafness in Children's Books	$3.00
Ageism in Children's Books	$3.00

Please add $1.00 for postage and handling

From Day Care and Child Development Council, 1012 14th Street N.W., Washington, D.C. 20005

STARTING OUT RIGHT: Choosing Books About Black People for Young Children	$2.50

From Feminist Press, Box 334, Old Westbury, N.Y. 11568

CATALOG listing many feminist books and resources	Free with SASE

From International Association of Business Communicators, 870 Market St., San Francisco, CA. 94102

WITHOUT BIAS: A Guidebook for Nondiscriminatory Communication	$4.00

From KNOW, Inc. Box 86031, Pittsburgh, PA. 15221

    YOU WON'T DO: What Textbooks on Government Teach High School Girls $1.50

    CATALOG   Free

From MacMillan Publishing Company, 866 Third Avenue,
    New York, N.Y. 10022

    GUIDELINES FOR CREATING POSITIVE SEXUAL AND RACIAL IMAGES IN EDUCATIONAL MATERIALS   Free

From Mayfield Publishing Company, 285 Hamilton Avenue,
    Palo Alto, CA. 94301

    SEX ROLE SOCIALIZATION by Lenore J. Weitzman $3.95

From McGraw-Hill Book Company, 1221 Avenue of the Americas,
    New York, N.Y. 10020

    GUIDELINES FOR EQUAL TREATMENT OF THE SEXES   Free

From Random House, 201 East 50th St., New York, N.Y. 10022

    RANDOM HOUSE GUIDELINES for MULTI/ETHNIC NONSEXIST SURVEY   Free

From U.S. Commission on Civil Rights, Washington, D.C. 20425

    CHARACTERS IN TEXTBOOKS: A Review of the Literature   Free

    FAIR TEXTBOOKS: A Resource Guide   Free

From Women on Words and Images, P.O. Box 2163,
    Princeton, N.J. 08540

    HELP WANTED: Sexism in Career Education Materials $2.50

    CATALOG   Free with SASE